PUBLISHING POETRY

The Essential Guide

Need
– 2 –
Know

First published in Great Britain in 1998 by Writers' Bookshop.
Writers' Bookshop is an imprint of Forward Press Ltd.

Second Edition published in Great Britain in 2010 by
Need2Know
Remus House
Coltsfoot Drive
Peterborough
PE2 9JX
Telephone 01733 898103
Fax 01733 313524
www.need2knowbooks.co.uk

Need2Know is an imprint of Forward Press Ltd.
www.forwardpress.co.uk
SB ISBN 978-1-86144-113-3
Cover photographs: Dreamstime

Contents

Introduction 5

Chapter 1 Getting There From Here 7

Chapter 2 Getting a Name in the Journals 13

Chapter 3 Readings 25

Chapter 4 Foreign Bodies: Publishing Abroad 33

Chapter 5 Preparing a Collection 39

Chapter 6 Marketing 57

Chapter 7 A Checklist for Poets 69

Chapter 8 Afterword 81

Help List 85

Book List 93

Introduction

It's probably true to say that at no time before have so many people been writing poetry. There are poems written on buses, poems read on the radio, poems on the Internet, poems displayed in shop windows.

But it's also probably true to say that never before have so many people been trying desperately to gain an audience for their poetry. More often than not, many of them end up miserable because they don't really know how to start.

This book shows you how you can beat the odds and see your work in print – and gain a financial reward into the bargain. It takes courage, much determination, a bit of luck and a poet who's already producing good pieces of work. This book aims to encourage at every turn; to provide you with a variety of ideas so you can succeed in the poetry business and achieve your ambitions despite all that the gloom merchants tell you.

First and foremost, though, you must believe in your own work. You must believe that your poetry is worth something, that you have things to say which matter, which are just that bit different to all the elegies and sonnets and haikus that have been written before. You must believe in your writing (while still being able to listen to genuinely constructive criticism), however hard that may prove at times.

This book will provide you, I hope, with a map and compass. It cannot give you all the signposts nor tell you what to do at every junction, for each road will be different and difficult in its own way. What I do hope is that it may make the journey easier.

'First and foremost, you must believe in your own work. You must believe that your poetry is worth something, that you have things to say which matter.'

Chapter One

Getting There From Here

William Golding's first novel was *The Lord of the Flies* – it won him the Nobel Prize. A screenplay can be dashed off by a novice and snapped up by Warner Brothers the following summer. It can happen. But many writers, even experienced ones, don't realise that a different methodology is required to get a first collection of poems published.

So, why should poetry be different to other genres?

Well, to begin with, there is very rarely a large pot of gold for a new poet. That's not to say that there isn't money around for poets, but it is fair to say it's harder to come by and in less generous quantities. Those who do invariably profit from these winnings are the well-known poets, the 'names.'

If you are at the top of the tree in poetry, or at least already up in the higher branches, publishing a collection will be much easier. A new collection by Heaney will sell at least 30,000 copies. A new poet's work and reputation is likely to be absolutely unknown to a publisher. Because of this they will almost certainly reject a collection from that poet, no matter how good the work may be. So how on earth do you see those poems in print?

The answer is you have to prove to a publisher that you have what it takes to be on their list of poets. You have to show your muscles and your medals. This means you have to have a good CV as a poet, i.e. your work must be published widely in journals and newspapers here in Britain and preferably overseas as well.

'You have to prove to a publisher that you have what it takes to be on their list of poets. You have to show your muscles and your medals.'

You have to have plucked up the courage to undertake literary readings of your work, because poetry publishers are well aware of the fact that often many more poetry books sell at such events than in bookshops. In short, you have to be good at marketing yourself in this cynical age when economic viability, not classical idealism, is what publishers want.

To begin with, you have to have a belief in your own poetry. I don't just mean that you must be convinced it is great – that's not sufficient. When you have got a small collection of poems together, let a select circle of people read and evaluate them. Don't choose 'yes-men'; there's no point being told your work is brilliant by friends and family who'd hate to disappoint you.

Choose people who will give you an honest evaluation, who have some kind of an appreciation of literature or who are involved themselves in the writing/publishing world. If all of them say your work needs honing, the chances are it does. If the majority feel you are wonderful at poems that describe your inner state but not nearly so good at portraying rural landscapes, then concentrate on that strong side. Often other people's insights will reveal to you truths you yourself would never have seen.

Writers' groups

This is why a writers' group can be a boon. If there is one in your area, then consider going along at least for a time. This may well provide you with a chance to read your work to a small audience and to hear their reactions. You may also be lucky enough to meet like-minded people with whom you can share ideas and projects, and from whom you can gain encouragement.

But join a writers' group with caution. Some well-established clubs become like families; either they praise each other's work without ever daring to pass negative comment, or else they are only too eager to pour scorn on newcomers' work in a snobbish manner.

I ran away from a writers' group when I was a tender teenager; it was dominated by a retired colonel who damned every piece of writing he didn't personally approve of. Writers' groups can seriously damage your health;

tread carefully and if in doubt, leave. A writers' group can be a help, but it can also be a hindrance. I'm still not an active member of one and I don't feel I've suffered one bit!

Mind your language

A word on language at the very outset. Obviously different poets have different styles, just like any other writers, but the language we use has to be looked at carefully.

In the first instance, I'm talking about archaic language versus contemporary language. Quite often when I'm marking competitions I come across entries full of 'ere' and 'whither,' 'thou' and 'maiden.' It's not a good idea to do this, quite simply because we don't go around using Shakespeare's English unless we happen to be acting in one of his plays.

Your language can be dignified and poetic, but it should not contain stereotypical words that are just not used in common speech or writing today. The only exception to this might be if you are writing a historical poem, recreating, let us say, the last words of Mary Queen of Scots before she faced her executioners. But even here you don't need to attempt to adopt old-fashioned language; just look at W.H. Auden's famous poem on the Roman soldier in Britain and you'll see what I mean.

The other important thing I want to mention concerns swearing and blasphemy. Contemporary literature has pushed back the boundaries of what is acceptable to the very limits, so some infamous novels come across more as a flow of swearwords than much else. The problem is that if you use strong language to that extent, it loses its impact on the reader and becomes redundant. My advice to you is to think very carefully before using strong language of any kind in your poetry. Ask yourself why you are using it. Is there a significance behind it or are you simply trying to be trendy? As long as you can justify your use of strong language convincingly there is not a real problem, but make sure you know where you stand on this before you run into criticism.

'Your language can be dignified and poetic, but it should not contain stereotypical words that are just not used in common speech or writing today.'

Reading

It's probably true to say that at no time before have so many people been writing. Part of that's to do with the greater amount of free time that we have, and also the interest that has sprung up in providing greater leisure services for the retired. More people, too, are aware of the potential rewards to be gained from writing blockbusters, bodice rippers and biographies.

In the poetry world, things are no different. There are literally hundreds of small press poetry magazines and journals in Britain alone, and new ones spring up every week.

The problem is that people are, by and large, writing more than they are reading. I know I've often been guilty of this myself and still have to push myself to read my weekly quota of prose and poetry. But reading is vitally important. As writers, we need to know what is being published and what succeeds. We also need to read the poetry and prose of yesteryear, which has been adjudged to be great. We may be certain we want to write free verse, but understanding the magic of the sonnet and being able to produce rhyming couplets is no bad thing. I've often been told by art teachers that the best painters are always first-class drawers too. As a child, you need to be able to walk before you can run.

So, as poets, we have to work at this reading business. We need to read the contemporary stuff as well as the classic stuff, even if we don't much care for it. New poetry books are often very expensive, so take advantage of your library service and order Wendy Cope's latest collection, the collected poems of John Masefield, or a brand new volume by Simon Armitage.

Try to subscribe to one or two poetry magazines to find out what their likes and dislikes are. If you can, visit the South Bank Centre in London or the Poetry Library in Edinburgh to browse through a whole range of past and present publications.

Sometimes it may be very tempting to live in that ivory tower of poetry, but ultimately it won't do us any good. You have to be able to speak with authority about what your likes and dislikes are in contemporary poetry, and you have to know the work of the top literary outlets so you can stand a chance of getting published there.

Need2Know

Don't stop reading

As I stressed in the opening chapter, building up a reputation in the literary magazines and journals is of fundamental importance to a poet starting out. But where do you begin? There are literally hundreds of magazines catering for poets in Great Britain, ranging from the big glossies like *Poetry Wales* or *Agenda*, to stapled together pamphlets produced in attics and garages. How do you know the great from the small before you start?

I have attempted to compile a directory of some of the most reliable journals in Britain and abroad at the back of this book, but if you want a comprehensive picture you will really need to subscribe to a whole range of magazines or visit the Poetry Library in London. Sometimes writers' groups will have a library of poetry books and journals as a resource for their members, but this will be more a case of luck than anything else. You also need to keep searching on the Internet – new magazines are appearing all the time.

I myself never saw any journals at all when I started out. I fired work blindly at everything from *Poetry Review* to *Planet*, working on the principle that if you throw sufficient mud, some of it has to stick in the end. Once I had work accepted, I was of course sent a copy of the journal, so bit by bit I built up a picture of the scene. It's one way of doing it, but I don't recommend the process.

'Don't stop reading, however successful you become.'

Questions to ask yourself

When you pick up a journal or magazine, try to analyse it:

- Does it like poetry using form or rhyme?
- Does it favour work of a more urban, gritty nature?
- Is it particularly keen to support writing by women poets?
- Is it cutting edge or quite likely to print traditional material, even accepting sonnets and poems using old forms?
- Does it request a certain style of poetry?

Summing Up

- Learn how to market yourself – you need to prove to an editor that you are passionate about poetry by getting a name for yourself.

- Believe in your poetry, but also get feedback from reputable sources.

- Build up a reputation in the literary magazines and journals – find out where and who to contact.

- Start immersing yourself in poetry magazines and journals – new issues and back issues. Visit the Poetry Library, search online, subscribe.

Chapter Two
Getting a Name in the Journals

The journals

It may be that as an unknown poet you will be fortunate enough to get writing straight into *Poetry Review*, *Poetry London*, *Agenda* or *Magma*. But quite frankly, like everywhere else, reputation helps. It is certainly said that trying to get work taken for outlets like the *London Review of Books* or the *Times Literary Supplement* is pretty hopeless unless you are already known. So starting here is hardly advisable.

Where to start

I advise beginning with a mixture of the very small magazines and one or two of the middle-ranking journals. At the beginning, what you need more than anything else is confidence, and getting into any of these magazines will give you a rightful feeling of success. It will also provide you with a very important commodity – friends.

Once you have built up confidence with the smaller outlets and can face the slings and arrows of the big boys, try your luck with them (but be prepared for the rejection slips). The best hope you can have of getting published in a literary magazine is to sense an awareness of what they're looking for. Do they have a Guardian-esque social edge? Is the journal fond of well-sculpted work inspired by nature? Are women writers particularly welcomed? Do you see sonnets, haikus and villanelles here? Firing into the dark is as good as useless; becoming acquainted with the magazines where you dream of seeing your work in print is simple good sense.

It goes without saying that from now on, you have to accept the day-to-day reality of rejection slips. All poets have to get used to them, and even the greats go on suffering them. One of my friends, who runs a small magazine near Glasgow, told me he rejected some of Seamus Heaney's poems just before the poet received his Nobel Prize. I could paper the house, let alone a room, with the rejection slips I've received.

Some rejections hurt more than others. But you have to remember that there are several reasons for material being unacceptable – it's not automatically true that your work was just bad. It may have been bad timing; maybe an issue had newly been completed and the editor didn't want to stock-pile more material right away. Perhaps poems on a very similar theme to yours had just been accepted, maybe it was just a bad day.

A standard rejection slip says little at all, but don't assume the worst about your work and throw your laptop into the Thames. Bear in mind that a big literary magazine like *Poetry Review* may receive upwards of 30,000 unsolicited poems a year. That's right, 30,000. That makes 600 poems a week. Don't let odds like that make you give up, but bear in mind nonetheless that the competition is stiff and that many factors can come into play to decide whether or not your poems make it.

More magazines and journals are appearing all the time – both printed and online – so keep doing your research and keep trawling through the Internet.

'From now on, you have to accept the day-to-day reality of rejection slips. All poets have to get used to them, and even the greats go on suffering them.'

The covering letter

Many poets seem to think this is an unnecessary addition to a submission of poems, almost a waste of time. Experience tells me that this assumption is quite wrong; a covering letter, or email if the outlet allows you to submit electronically, can do a great deal to aid the reception your poems get. A friendly introduction will do your chances no harm. Perhaps the six poems you are submitting were all inspired by a study tour to Eastern Europe, or by a visit to Gaelic-speaking communities in Ireland – if so, then mention that. It gives you, the poet, a human face, preparing the way for the editor's reading of your work.

Of course, it's possible to damage your reception by enclosing an essay, not a letter. There is no need to antagonise a busy editor by going into great detail, describing the latest weather in Skegness. You will find your own perfect covering letter in the end; the one I use to new magazines takes me all of half a minute to write now – it is so deeply engrained in my pen!

Your letters will change as you get to know individual editors who have used your work before. This is one of the spin-offs of working as a freelance writer; by and by you find real friends among the editors of magazines you write for. There are perhaps a dozen editors between Cornwall and Cape Wrath I would happily call on if I happened to be passing, such is the rapport we've built up over the years. At any rate, overleaf is the kind of letter I used when I was starting out.

The first thing to note from the content of the letter is the use of the editor's name. Try to find this out, by hook or by crook, because it establishes a more personal contact and also looks as if you've done your homework on the magazine. Secondly, make mention of any kind of track record your poems have. Even if none have been published, then mention that a number of people have been encouraging your writing and urging you to get some of it published.

Later on, when your poetry has appeared in various journals around the country, mention perhaps three or four in a covering letter, but don't list all 26. It's obviously counter-productive to appear arrogant to an editor you're trying to appeal to.

The submission

Whether you are submitting to an online or printed journal or magazine, before you submit any poems, try to visit the website of the outlet to become familiar with their submission guidelines. Read the magazine or journal too so you can get a feel for their style – online if you can, or pick up a copy from your local library, bookshop or writers' group.

Peter Roberts
Rose Cottage
Waterside Lane
Liverpool
L4 ZYT

Louise Taylor
Editor
Boom Magazine
Liverpool

20th July 2010

Dear Louise Taylor,

Please find enclosed six fairly recent poems which I'd ask you to consider for *Boom*.

They were written while I was still working as a geologist for British Nuclear Fuels in Wales and concern many of my own thoughts on the industry at that time.

Several of my poems were recently used on local radio here in Liverpool and the feedback from listeners was very positive.

I look forward to hearing from you in due course.

Yours sincerely,

Peter Roberts

Peter Roberts

In general, each submission should contain perhaps between five and eight poems. It can contain fewer, but definitely not a greater number than that. Only one poem should appear on a single page of A4, and at all costs get access to a laptop rather than writing your poetry out by hand.

In the past I used to advise writers to send a stamped addressed envelope with their submission. However, as we all have the facility to store documents electronically, there really is no need.

Anthologies

Every year, new poetry anthologies appear across Britain and indeed across the world. The first thing to point out is that a number of these are in fact run by vanity operators, i.e. people who aren't going to pay you for your poem but ask you to pay for the privilege of seeing it in print. Don't touch them with a barge pole, and tell everyone else not to into the bargain. You can sniff out vanity publishers of anthologies easily after a bit of practice; they promise, for example, to publish the work of 200 poets in a volume entitled *Flowers of the Golden Children*, and this will be available to you at the 'specially reduced rate of £29.95, and available with a mahogany cover...'

However, many worthy publishers produce high quality anthologies, often on countryside topics or featuring authors from a particular region or background. The anthologies compiled by Forward Press in Peterborough (www.forwardpress.co.uk) have proved particularly successful, and have helped many frustrated poets see their work in print for the first time (see help list for details).

Every year anthologies will be looking for poetry. The best way to find out about them is to check with poetry libraries and also with local libraries too. Keep your eyes peeled for genuine adverts requesting poets to submit their work, and keep checking the websites of reputable publishers for submission information (you could perhaps make a list and check off regularly). There are new opportunities for anthology outlets all the time: local, national and international.

'Keep your eyes peeled for genuine adverts requesting poets to submit their work, and keep checking the websites of reputable publishers for submission information. There are new opportunities for anthology outlets all the time.'

Cassell (now part of Orion Books) used to produce anthologies on various topics – and a couple of years ago an American publisher took one of my poems for an anthology on herons! Every year New Writing Scotland produces an anthology of previously unpublished poetry and short stories from writers in Scotland. Some of the larger literary publishers do the same in England; it might focus on women's writing, on people's reactions to the war in Iraq, on the death of Michael Jackson, and so on.

Find copies of anthologies like these in bookshops and take a note of them. Write to these publishers and ask if they are planning further such titles and, if so, what type of poetry they are looking for. In the beginning, half the battle is knowing what is going on where; it is about keeping your ear to the ground and picking up on every available opportunity. Luck does play a part, but so does sheer, dogged Holmes and Watson sleuthing.

'Anthologies matter because they look good mentioned in your CV and thus increase your standing, and because many of them pay fairly generously for the work they accept.'

Anthologies matter because they look good mentioned in your CV and thus increase your standing, and because many of them pay fairly generously for the work they accept.

Writers' group anthologies can also be useful, but many are let down by poor production standards, bad editing and amateurish design quality. If you are going to do a thing, do it well. Make sure the editing is carried out strictly and meticulously, and make sure the finished product looks as good as it possibly could. What is the point of wasting tremendous writing with rotten production? But a good-looking, well-written anthology can do both a group's and an individual poet's reputation no harm at all.

Competitions

Another way of building up your literary CV to boost your chances of having a full collection accepted is by entering poetry competitions.

You will see these advertised everywhere from supermarkets to undergrounds, the reason being that poetry competitions make a considerable amount of money for the people who run them. The average entry fee for the major competitions today is £5 per poem, so if the organisers receive 5,000 poems, they should have plenty left over after awarding a few thousand to the winner and a few runners-up prizes.

Winners of the most prestigious contests often go on to become well-known published poets: Don Paterson, Kathleen Jamie and Jo Shapcott are just three whose reputations were greatly enhanced by carrying off laurel wreaths in some of the majors.

Do beware, however, before pouring all your savings into the myriad of poetry competitions around the country. Have a look at the type of writing which is winning awards at the moment. Much of this trendy poetry is concerned with inner-city realism and the harshness of the world we live in today; poems about flocks of swans or golden daffodils are less likely to win prizes.

Bearing this general point in mind, do consider each competition carefully on its merits. In time you will get a sense of the literary likes and dislikes of individual judges, and can decide whether or not it's worth forking out a fiver for an entry.

I personally prefer the smaller, more local, contests to the giants. The odds of winning a prize are higher because the organisers, with less money to spend on advertising, will have received fewer entries. The big boys (and girls) of the poetry world are also less likely to bother entering.

In addition, entry fees tend to be more reasonable; you might pay £1 or £2 per poem, but not more. In such competitions, you might find a first prize of perhaps £600; not to be sneezed at by any writer struggling to make ends meet!

Writing competitions in general are a bit like gambling. You're sure the piece you're entering is going to win and you're willing to put your money where your mouth is. Most of the time you get it wrong, but once every so often if you're lucky your hunch proves to be right.

But luck is the operative word. Judging competitions is a highly subjective business. I know because I'm often asked to do it myself, and struggle to keep as open a mind as possible. But I'm fully aware that like any other judge, I'm drawn to the type of work I like best and for which I will have an inbuilt preference.

So enter competitions in strict moderation, and now and again use that tenner, instead, to buy a second-hand copy of Wallace Stevens' poetry or a ticket to a reading by Seamus Heaney. I know which option will do your poetry more good....

(A list of some of the poetry competitions to watch out for will be found at the end of this book.)

Simultaneous submissions

Many poets beginning to send their writing out for the first time rightly wonder if they should send the same poems to two or more outlets at the one time.

My own attitude is that magazines have no reason to expect that poets will dutifully wait until they have a response from the first outlet before sending the same work to the second. A poet's lot is not an easy one. If Smedley from *Colussus* sits on your very best material for half a year and more, why should you not have the right to allow Simons from *Taurus* to see the same poems and make a decision in two months?

'Do send your new, great poem to several outlets at the one time. But remember to keep a careful record of where each poem has travelled and don't get caught out.'

If magazines want to be treated with the respect they feel they are due, then they have to begin by treating their writers fairly. I appreciate that many editors receive groaning postbags day in, day out, but that gives them no excuse to lose material or to return it many months later with coffee stains and crossings-out.

So do send your new, great poem to several outlets at the one time. But remember to keep a careful record of where each poem has travelled and don't get caught out. The danger is if two big magazines (who will know each other's publications well) both accept the same poem. You will be extremely unpopular if the piece appears in both, and you even risk being blacklisted. You will certainly face problems ever getting these two outlets to accept your poetry again.

If for some reason this does happen, don't do nothing. You must decide which of the two is going to be of more benefit to you in the long run. Then you will have to write to the other and apologise profusely for your error and withdraw your poem there and then. With any luck you will be forgiven and the editor will bear no grudge against you.

However, if your poem is accepted for *Poetry Review* and for the *Diddlebury Women's Institute Quarterly*, I wouldn't worry unduly. The chances are that the editor of *Poetry Review* is not an avid reader of the *Diddlebury Women's Institute Quarterly*!

Waiting for a reply

How long do you sit impatiently waiting for that editor's reply? The answer is really in your own hands, but it is not a good idea to start phoning up a fortnight after submitting poems to find out what the reaction was.

Editors may not always be as busy as they claim to be, but busy they certainly are, and attempting to cajole them into a decision will only have one result. Believe me, I've been there. Never phone a poetry editor, that's my advice. Not unless you know this individual very well and have found him or her to be in constant good spirits. Phone, perhaps, to ask about when your work is to appear or about the cheque which should have arrived and hasn't, but don't ring up to demand news of your last submission. It doesn't look good.

If weeks and months have rolled by since you submitted work and you can justify asking for news, then drop the editor a postcard or short email. But make it as friendly as possible and keep the tone light. Playing with a lion's tail is always dangerous.

The best cure for impatience is to send out new work somewhere else. Keep the pot boiling; then you will not be waiting for one vital reply and a possible big disappointment.

Keeping a record of your work

If you intend to take up this battle seriously, then you need to be organised about it. Be a Byron by night, but do your homework by day. It will pay dividends.

In a notebook, make a list of the outlets you have sent poetry to. When I do this, I mention after each magazine title the individual poems it has received; in this way there isn't a danger of sending any outlet the same work over again. It also means I can have an overview of what poems are 'on the market' and which are 'on the shelf.'

At any one time, I will have anywhere between 100 and 150 poems being considered by journals. But even if you have only 10 or 12 pieces doing the rounds, you need to ensure you have a note of where they are. Beside each submission listing I leave a space so that I can either place a tick there if one or more poems is accepted, or more usually a cross when I have been unsuccessful. I list my submissions month by month so that I can also look back to see how long ago it was since I inflicted work on *The Scrooge* or had yet another crack at getting into *Missing Link*. I also dutifully note my income because eventually poetry earnings can come to interest the taxman.

I also strongly urge you to keep another notebook where you can store the names of useful contacts, magazines and publishers you discover by chance, the addresses of competitions, etc. If you're serious about this, you will over time become a detective, with your poetry spectacles rarely far away. If you go to readings or are leafing through magazines and flyers at your local bookshop, then have this notebook to hand so you can make a note of any new information that might help your cause. Once you are conducting your own readings, you also need to be on the look out for adverts for writers' groups and literary gatherings, where a poet might prove to be a very welcome guest.

All this may seem fussy and not very important, but, as they say, it takes many droplets to make the ocean.

'At any one time, I will have anywhere between 100 and 150 poems being consid- ered by journals. But even if you have only 10 or 12 pieces doing the rounds, you need to ensure you have a note of where they are.'

Summing Up

▪ When it comes to sending out your poetry, start with the small magazines and slowly build up to the larger ones. Build your contacts and your reputation step-by-step.

▪ Don't take rejection letters personally; you have to accept the reality of rejection slips. All poets receive them!

▪ Before you submit poetry to a magazine or journal, ensure you become familiar with their submission guidelines. Become well acquainted with the outlet; what do they publish? What is their angle? What advice do they give poets?

▪ Anthologies: do your research. Look out for genuine adverts for submission, read writing magazines for latest submissions and regularly visit reputable poetry publishers' websites for calls to submit.

▪ If you are sending multiple submissions out, make sure you keep a record of where and when you have sent your work.

Chapter Three

Readings

I think many aspiring poets look on readings much the same as most mortals look on dental appointments. I know I did to begin with, and I still find visits to secondary schools rather like having to cross crocodile-infested water.

But there's no way round this if you want to stand a serious chance of having a collection taken on by a publisher. I reiterate that most poetry books sell through readings, not through bookshops, and publishers are as aware of that fact as poets.

You don't need to book the Albert Hall for your first venue. Small is beautiful, and small in this case is also less intimidating. You must at all costs aim to build your confidence, not to destroy it altogether.

A few years back when I finally accepted the awful truth about having to do readings, I undertook one in the town of Paisley outside Glasgow. Quite blithely I took along all my poems of country and coast, never considering what type of material would be presented by the other invited poets. The man before me read a delightful prose poem about the murder of an old man and his little dog, and the poems that had come before were all concerned with gang violence, drugs and general cruelty. I felt like getting up when it was my turn and saying, 'Look, I shouldn't be here at all. I'll come back some other time. Bye.' But it was too late for that. My poems went down like lead weights in a duck pond. I crawled off the stage in tatters and it was a long time before I had the confidence to read again.

'I reiterate that most poetry books sell through readings, not through bookshops, and publishers are as aware of that fact as poets.'

Starting out

To begin with then, make very sure that you're comfortable with the people you're reading with and the kind of environment you have as a venue.

Later on, once you have built up your confidence and know that you can present your poetry and present it well, this will be far less of a consideration. I have enough wisdom to steer clear of some very specific inner city events, but I rarely turn down an opportunity to read.

I suggest that you do a reading first with either one person or with a group of folk whose work you know and who have given encouragement to your own poetry in the past. They may be members of your writers' group, or they might be contributors to one of the magazines in which your work has also appeared.

'I suggest that you do a reading first with either one person or with a group of folk whose work you know and who have given encouragement to your own poetry in the past.'

I suggest this because undertaking the whole programme alone to start with is a tall order. Apart from anything else, it requires reading a great number of poems! If you read as part of a larger circle, you yourself are likely to be able to choose how many pieces you will present. Even having the opportunity to read two or three short poems will give you a first important injection of confidence.

Preparation

I've been at many readings where poets got up on the stage and began, 'I've... er...got a couple of...well...poems I wrote quite a long time ago, actually. They are...er...you know, things I felt quite strongly about, actually.'

I'm not just writing this to be nasty, I'm writing it because I felt extremely sorry for the poets concerned. This is not how to get the public on your side, nor how to create an impression. This is not how to sell yourself, or to sell books.

Now I am no born orator, believe me. I am softly spoken, and after long and horrible years at school, I don't have a vast amount of confidence. It's obvious that the poets who began their reading like that had very little confidence too, but then that's all the more reason to go prepared!

I never undertake a reading without having gone through in my head what I'm going to present. I write down the gist of my programme so that I know the order of things and can work out roughly how long I will speak for. (If you're told to read for an hour and you dry up after 10 minutes, you're in trouble, and vice versa.)

Here is some practical advice to get you started:

- If you can, find a quiet place at home where you can rehearse your programme.

- Try to memorise the gist of it so you don't have to read from the paper but rather use what you've written as notes.

- If you can, think of a couple of funny comments to begin your programme; it will give you confidence and will make the audience warm at once to you and what you have to say.

- Make an ironic comment about your nervous state, about the fact that this may be your first and last reading, etc. It's good policy to build up a little stock of stories which you can use to warm up audiences.

I'm not suggesting you have to become a stand-up comedian, but melting the ice is always of value, and such an approach will always help you through those first five dreadful minutes, in particular.

Looking good

I suppose this is a subjective point, but I reckon it's worth looking your best at a poetry reading. Some poets turn up in torn jeans and a rather sheepy pullover. Now don't get me wrong, most of my friends fall into the sheepy category, indeed I would consider myself pretty sheepy. But if you want to be taken seriously as a writer, then you have to look serious about it. I know that Wendy Cope makes a point of wearing a suit at her readings because she considers poetry to be her professional career, and as a result she wants to be businesslike in the way she approaches it.

I think it's important, too, because a large sector of society thinks poets, like all artists, get up for lunch, shave at Christmas and smoke roll-ups. The stereotype is amusing, but the treatment some people give artists is not. It's worth working to try to change that perception in society.

I'm not suggesting that everyone contemplating undertaking readings should go out and buy a complete new wardrobe at vast expense. Nor am I suggesting that you have to look as 'businesslike' as Wendy Cope. If someone put a tie round my neck before a reading, I'd think I was back at school and

'At all costs, feel comfortable with what you choose to wear. Feel attractive, because this in turn will give you confidence when it is your turn to stand up to read.'

go to pieces. At all costs, feel comfortable with what you choose to wear. Feel attractive, because this in turn will give you confidence when it is your turn to stand up to read.

Going solo

When you begin to climb that poetry ladder and you are at last invited to do solo readings, organise things before-hand as much as you can.

'Often you will meet important people at readings; important in the sense that they can offer new leads, assistance to get on. And struggling poets have to grab every chance they can.'

If you feel more confident with a lectern then arrange to have one at the venue. (I recommend that you stand to read; older people in particular will grumble about not hearing sufficiently well, and your voice will carry better if you are on your feet.) Have a glass of water near at hand, not vodka. After half an hour in an airless hall, your throat will feel like the runway at Heathrow, and as a poet you have to look after that throat of yours. But avoid alcohol before you begin; it's dangerous to start relying on a quick whisky 'to calm the nerves' every time. Reward yourself afterwards, not before.

If you are the sole reader, I suggest you speak for about three-quarters of an hour. If the audience is a school one, cut that to half an hour. There's no point reading to an inattentive audience or one that is starting to think about the tea and buns. I once read at a large conference on publishing poetry abroad, and after an hour I noticed that several elderly ladies had fallen asleep. It did not do my confidence much good.

If you have books out by this time, or information about your readings, make sure this is clearly displayed at the venue. It's also a good idea to suggest to your publisher that they make flyers available; if you keep them in the loop with your publicity, they may be able to help.

After people have asked questions – if you want them to ask questions – inform them of the availability of publicity materials, books or whatever. It's worth having a clipboard and pen on your display table so that those interested in your work can be put on a mailing list. This means that when a book comes out, or a reading takes place in a certain area, you can target the individuals most likely to be interested.

Finally, after all readings, keep your ear to the ground. Don't vanish out of the hall like a scalded cat, stay to talk to people. It may be that you meet some eccentrics who want to know what your opinion is of Shelley's Queen Mab or the last part of some remote sonnet of Shakespeare's. But it may also be that Lady Denisa of Marlberry House wonders if you would be able to give a reading for her house party on Christmas Eve. Often you will meet important people at readings; important in the sense that they can offer new leads, assistance to get on. And struggling poets have to grab every chance they can.

The content

Obviously, over time you will work out yourself the most successful format for your own readings. You will hear other poets presenting their work and learn what is successful in their programmes – as well as what is utterly dreadful! (I have listened to several extremely respected poets in the last years and in the main their presentations left an awful lot to be desired. I'm not sure whether that is comforting for us or worrying!)

Read poems slowly, don't go through them as if you have a train to catch. Poetry is 'deep language' – an audience needs time to absorb metaphor and imagery, to grasp meaning. If you can, give even a brief introduction to individual poems.

It always annoyed me when pop groups I loved just ploughed on with their programmes, giving no background information about what inspired one particular song or another. I knew something important must have been behind classic lyrics and melodies, and I wanted to have at least an inkling of the secret. Dare to share a little of yourself with an audience – they will want to know all the more.

> 'Read poems slowly, don't go through them as if you have a train to catch. Poetry is "deep language" – an audience needs time to absorb metaphor and imagery, to grasp meaning.'

Finance

There are costs involved in organising and running any event, and a reading is no exception. Normally there is the hire of the hall to be considered, the expenditure on refreshments, publicity costs and your own expenses. So if you are planning to organise your own reading, remember there is little point running an event which is going to prove a significant drain on your own resources.

Whether acting alone or as part of a group, try at all costs to obtain financial support for the event. In the first instance, contact the Arts Council (find your local office) to see if they can help; it may be that the regional section will prove the most likely sponsors. The best bet is to do your homework as far in advance as possible; the Arts Council will send you detailed forms with questions concerning the event, and you will need to be clued up about your whole programme.

If you can include the reading in an arts festival then so much the better as it is likely they will carry the costs for your event, in addition to paying fees to the poets. You also stand a much better chance of getting a good audience, since the event will be listed in the festival programme.

If neither of these options proves possible then approach your council for advice. Because of the severe cuts in public spending of recent years, most councils are reluctant to finance so much as a tiddlywinks competition. All the same, they will have a local arts programme, and exist to provide advice and assistance to individuals and groups in the district. They may at least provide a venue and some advertising for your event.

'Whether acting alone or as part of a group, try at all costs to obtain financial support for the event. In the first instance, contact the Arts Council to see if they can help; it may be that the regional section will prove the most likely sponsors.'

Summing Up

■ Readings are essential if you want to have a chance at having a collection taken on by a publisher.

■ More poetry books are sold through readings than in bookshops.

■ Build up to reads. Start off with a friendly audience of friends from your writing group, fellow poets and colleagues to build your confidence.

■ Preparation is key, so plan your performance in advance. Read your poems slowly, and try to give a brief introduction to each poem. Give the audience some information about yourself.

■ Don't disappear as soon as your reading is over. People will want to talk and ask questions, and this is the ideal opportunity to create contacts and future leads.

■ You might be invited to do a poetry reading by another organiser, or you might decide to organise your own poetry reading, in which case you must consider the financial aspect of the equation.

Chapter Four

Foreign Bodies: Publishing Abroad

Getting published abroad as a poet is not by any means a prerequisite. There are so many top quality British literary outlets that you could quite happily spend a lifetime getting into them, without ever troubling to conquer the North American and Antipodean ones.

But there are several worthwhile reasons for trying all the same. The first has, once again, to do with gaining a reputation. Word of publication in a Canadian or Irish literary outlet will do your CV no harm at all, and will show an editor that you are willing to go far (literally) to win credits.

The second reason is a financial one. Although sending poetry abroad can be an expensive business if sending via post, it can also win you considerable rewards. Payment rates for journals supported by the Australia Council, for example, are generous, and the competition is definitely not as tough as in Britain.

It becomes a bit of an addiction, I suppose. Having got a poem into one particular journal, a copy of the publication duly arrives. In it you discover advertisements for three more outlets in the same country. Now you'll hardly be able to wait to try poems on these newly-discovered journals. The bug has got you...

Remember to keep a balance, all the same. Submitting work abroad is time-consuming and often frustrating. Information about outlets may be out-of-date and unreliable: editors' editorial addresses may have changed, the journal will perhaps have folded.

Checking information on British outlets can be difficult enough, but making sure all the details concerning a journal in Queensland are correct is another matter altogether.

Don't put all your eggs in one basket. Build up a steady knowledge of one or several journals abroad, and be faithful to these. Don't scatter poetry about the globe in a desperate bid to become famous overnight, because you will only be left frustrated and very out of pocket.

'Submitting work abroad is time-consuming and often frustrating. Information about outlets may be out of date and unreliable: editors' editorial addresses may have changed, the journal will perhaps have folded.'

Submitting poems

I have already mentioned the potential expense of sending poetry via the post to foreign journals. For that reason, you have to think of all ways possible to keep the cost of submissions to the minimum.

Now I am lucky in that most of my poems are short – on average between 12 and 15 lines in length. I know that you are often reminded to submit each poem on a separate sheet of paper, but when dealing with foreign outlets this would prove quite impossible. My solution is to put four or five separate poems onto two sides of an A4 sheet, thus saving a lot of paper and a lot of weight!

However, as mentioned earlier, always try to visit the website of the journal or magazine you are submitting to – you may find that they accept submissions online through their website or via email, thereby eliminating all costs. However, for some outlets this is not an option.

Often I choose poems which have been successful in Britain and which people have liked particularly. So I will submit poems published previously in this country, though whether that is strictly 'cricket' or not I don't know. I haven't been extradited yet.

Whether you are submitting by post or email, never miss out on a covering letter/email. This is just as important as with a submission to a British outlet, indeed it is perhaps even more vital. There is all the more need for a foreign editor to know 'where you are coming from.' If sending by mail, don't use a full sheet of A4 if you can help it; instead get hold of one of these small pads with postcard sized sheets. Obviously if you are going to be sending your work via email, you still need to include a short message with your attachments.

This might be a letter to a new outlet in Australia (you could easily convert into an email):

Peter Roberts
Rose Cottage
Waterside Lane
Liverpool
L4 ZYT

Steve Waters
Editor
The Poet Magazine
Sydney
Australia

16th August 2010

Dear Mr. Waters,

I heard of your journal recently, and I am submitting/attaching several poems for consideration. I apologise that all the work appears on one single sheet of A4, but this is the most effective way of submitting when postage is so expensive.

My poetry has appeared in a number of British journals and in *Back Beat* in Canberra. Many of my poems concern my years spent in the army and detail experiences in Northern Ireland and the Falkland Islands.

Yours sincerely

Peter Roberts

Peter Roberts

General points

At the end of the book I have included a small checklist of some of the outlets I have found success with. Obviously this is by no means exhaustive: if you are really keen to pursue this publishing line, then a book I have found extremely helpful is the *Poet's Market*. This is an American hardback book big enough to kill a horse. It contains listings of poetry outlets worldwide, but concentrates naturally enough on the North American journals. What is useful about this handbook is that it provides the reader with background information on each magazine: the standard of work accepted, the approximate time taken to deal with submissions, the type of writing particularly sought after, etc.

A word of caution though. The various outlets differ considerably from each other, and it is important to be aware of these differences. Try to evaluate which outlets seem most suitable for your poems, and which seem less appropriate in terms of style and level, particularly if you are starting out. Submitting poetry abroad is a much greater investment – often in terms of time as well as finance – so it is well worth stacking the odds as much in your favour as possible before you begin.

Now, in the past I used to include with every submission at least one International Reply Coupon, because obviously you can't send a stamped addressed envelope to Hawaii or Hong Kong. However, I now send away batches of poems and just ask that the editor sends me an email to let me know of his/her decision in the fullness of time. This saves the expense and trouble of IRCs. Now that we all have stored documents, there's no point having work mailed back.

A final point concerns money. Although you are unlikely to get rich quick from the profits of poems published abroad, you may well receive the odd helpful cheque in due time. However, bear in mind that most of these will be paid in dollars not pounds. Some of the truly large journals have the wherewithal to send sterling, but don't hold your breath. Because banks charge unbelievable amounts to cash foreign cheques, it is worth hanging on to cheques to cash two or more at one time. If you have a reasonably helpful bank, they may well be persuaded to make just one charge for all the cheques. Don't see your hard-earned rewards robbed by the bank!

'Submitting poetry abroad is a much greater investment – often in terms of time as well as finance – so it is well worth stacking the odds as much in your favour as possible before you begin.'

One word of caution, however, concerning the domestic poetry scene. Be very wary of those offering to publish your work on the Internet at great expense; always ensure you do your homework before parting with your hard-earned cash.

Copyright

Some poets starting out are paranoid that the magazine or publisher to whom they submit their work will steal their poems. It's an understandable anxiety, but there's no need to be too anxious.

If anything is in genuine danger in the writing world, it is ideas. If you have a particularly brilliant brainwave about making a documentary on starfish off Newfoundland or the inventor of the bicycle pump, and submit these ideas to a television company, then you might be concerned about that. Cases have been brought – and successfully – against companies who declined someone's work and then went off with the idea to develop it themselves.

I have never yet heard of a magazine or publisher stealing a poem. Why should they? If it is good enough, they are likely to be all too quick to tell you; if it is not, they will reject the poem. The only place I can imagine it being possible to steal a poem is via the Internet, where someone reads a particularly good piece on the screen, copies it and submits it to a journal as their own. But even that seems a pretty remote possibility.

If you are unconvinced by this and still want the security of formal copyright, then the easiest way to proceed is to post yourself the poem or poems concerned. The sealed envelope containing your work has been franked and can be produced as evidence in the event of someone pilfering your poems. The other even simpler solution is to write © and your name at the bottom of the last page of your typescript. No one will dare risk stealing your work if you are claiming it has been formally copyrighted. You could also ask that should your work be printed, this copyright symbol is included.

Unless otherwise stated, a magazine or publisher reproducing your poetry does not buy the copyright to the work. That remains with you, the author.

'I have never yet heard of a magazine or publisher stealing a poem. Why should they? If it is good enough, they are likely to be all too quick to tell you; if it is not, they will reject the poem.'

Summing Up

- Sending poetry aboard for foreign publication can benefit your reputation and your bank balance!

- Be sensible when it comes to submitting poetry – if it has to go via mail, make sure you keep costs down and do your research. Always check to see how the outlet prefers you to submit your poetry.

- Always do your research and read the submission guidelines.

Chapter Five
Preparing a Collection

Preparing a collection for publishers

Once you feel your poems have won their spurs and you can respond to all the possible demands publishers might make, then prepare for battle. It's difficult to say how many poems should make up a collection, because every publisher has different formats; thus a collection is really as long as a piece of string. This is not something to fret over, because any publisher seriously interested in taking on your work will tailor the collection according to their requirements.

It also depends to a certain extent on how you have put your collection together. The poems will probably either be all your best-known ones to date, the ones which have made most of a splash in the magazines and which have proved most popular with audiences, or else all those on one particular theme: poems concerned with the sea, with Africa, with the loss of a loved one, or whatever. With the second type, it is important that all the poems are of a fairly similar standard. It is tempting to put in extra pieces which mean a great deal to you – but that isn't necessarily enough to satisfy a critical editor. Don't put in anything which might bring down the overall quality of the collection.

I think it's no bad idea at this stage to make three or four copies of the work to give out to individuals whose opinions you trust and who will give you honest, not kind, reactions. Ask them to mark any poems they find particularly weak, and see if these doubts are shared independently by the others.

Sometimes it's very hard indeed to look objectively at your own work, particularly if the poems concerned have become very familiar to you. Don't ignore criticism or react badly to it. Take constructive criticism on board and look at your collection again in the light of it. Prune, if that is necessary, painful as it may be.

A good home

There are obviously differences between the major publishers of poetry, but a truly strong collection should be admired wherever it lands. Poets dream of Faber, but to be given a home there requires a top class reputation in literary circles and, I suspect, a small quantity of good fortune. Tastes, I feel, have changed since the days when Hughes and Heaney started out there; Faber's new poets write very differently to the old vanguard. I'm not sure that poems about foxes or gathering brambles would prove so acceptable now. Both Bloodaxe and Jonathan Cape like strong, contemporary voices.

I don't believe in being unduly polite to publishers; they are very seldom polite to poets. It may seem honourable to let one copy of your collection go the rounds until it finds a home, but you may also see precious years of your life drift by while you wait. Several of my poetry collections which were submitted to top publishers are now missing presumed dead, others lingered there for innumerable months until my patience gave out and I requested them to be returned. Even if they do come back of their own accord, typescripts are often dog-eared, their covers have coffee stains and their pages smudges of black ink. Publishers have feet of clay, and very wobbly clay at that.

Making advances

While not wanting to bend over backwards to please publishers, I do think it is worthwhile doing everything possible to safeguard a precious collection of poetry.

For this reason, if you are daring to approach one or several of the large publishers, send on a letter first (enclosing an s.a.e.) so that your work will not arrive totally unsolicited and you will ascertain the name of the poetry editor who will receive your work.

This latter point is of particular relevance. Large publishers with many divisions are rather like elephants: tusks, trunk, ears, tail, etc. It may take a long time for your typescript to get from ears to tail if you didn't get it there to begin with.

You don't need a long covering letter in the first instance, though. A brief statement of your achievements to date will do no harm. If your handwriting is sufficiently legible then don't go to all the trouble of typing a letter. The same short piece can be used for several publishers, but do not photocopy your letter, whether it is typewritten or otherwise. Editors were not born yesterday, and this sort of mass production will win you no favours.

The send off

When you get the all-clear from one or several publishing houses, complete your final preparations to the typescript and look forward to a long wait.

Whatever type of collection yours is, arrange the poems in the kind of order you would like to see in a finished book, and number the pages in pencil at the top right-hand corner. Don't go to enormous trouble over a cover, especially if you are also an artist, because the chances are this page will come back dismembered, and a lot of your precious labour wasted.

This goes for illustrations in general: never submit them at the beginning of the whole battle. Publishers like to do things their way, and they do not take kindly to being told by any author how they want their book to look. 'My sister Jenny's a great artist' is the kind of talk which turns editors dark purple with rage. You can mention the idea of illustrating your collection if it seems particularly relevant (i.e. if you yourself are a professional artist), but do not push the point because you will antagonise the editor at once.

I generally include a sheet after the title page giving a brief run-down on the poems in the collection: what magazines or anthologies they have appeared in at home or abroad, mention of pieces broadcast on radio, etc. This is worthwhile; it is all about establishing the credentials of your work, and the more you can mention to boost its track record, the better.

The covering letter you now write is of real importance. Obviously each one will be different, but the following example provides an outline of the possible content.

'Large publishers with many divisions are rather like elephants: tusks, trunk, ears, tail, etc. It may take a long time for your typescript to get from ears to tail if you didn't get it there to begin with.'

Peter Roberts
Rose Cottage
Waterside Lane
Liverpool
L4 ZYT

Hilary Westbrook
Editor
Romulus Press
London

27th September 2010

Dear Hilary Westbrook,

Thank you for your recent letter concerning my poetry collection - I have pleasure in sending this on to you now. There are 45 poems in the *Killing Time* collection; all of these were inspired by the Gulf War and by the experiences of my own best friend, who was severely injured in the conflict.

Almost all the poems have been published, either here or in America. The best-known piece, *Dead and Buried*, was actually used in a recent television documentary on Gulf War Syndrome. This poem, and several others in the collection, were also broadcast on radio some months ago.

I have undertaken a great number of readings across the country in the last months, and have found that audiences are both challenged and moved by the poems from *Killing Time* in particular. This does not apply solely to library audiences; I have also been asked to visit several schools in the region to read from the collection and to discuss issues raised by the poems with senior school groups.

I have no doubt that this collection would succeed. A great number of people have inquired about obtaining copies already, and one or two head teachers have expressed interest in using the collection as a class text.

At any rate, I hope you will react positively to the poems here, and I look forward to hearing from you in due course.

Yours sincerely,

Peter Roberts

Peter Roberts

'The covering letter you now write is of real importance.'

Acceptance and rejection

You would be extremely fortunate if your collection were to be accepted first time round. How wonderful if that were the norm, but it just isn't, often not even with authors who go on to become exceptionally well known.

A few years ago I met an American lady who was a famous children's author. She was fairly elderly, and during her life she had seen a staggering number of her books published. But what was still fresh in her mind was the fight she had had to get the first one into print. That children's book was rejected by 83 publishers before one said yes.

I hope it won't be that hard for you – I was certainly more fortunate. But I quote this example to show what tenacity you have to have if you really want to succeed, if you really believe your work deserves an audience. I have a rule with myself that whatever comes in rejected at breakfast-time is in the mail again by lunch-time. I do that because it keeps me buoyant; it means I am back in the fight and I have new hope of success. Sometimes doing that is far from easy and requires a tremendous amount of willpower. You will discover your own way to cope and to bounce back, but find it you must if you are serious about winning a place in the writing world.

Down to business

If you do get that letter of acceptance, enjoy the moment to the full. It is a magnificent feeling to get a book accepted for publication; a bit like being told your baby is going to be born!

But don't just wait in a sea of bliss until the finished product arrives. There's hard work ahead of you, and your input will help to ensure the best results. Publishers have a nasty habit of disappearing at this stage, of doing everything themselves so that the author has as little chance of sticking their oar in as possible.

'If you do get that letter of acceptance, enjoy the moment to the full. It is a magnificent feeling to get a book accepted for publication.'

A while back, I went to Edinburgh to meet the publishers of my latest poetry collection. I remember my shock when the editor took me over to the computer to show me the planned illustrations for the book. 'Do you think these will be all right?' she asked anxiously. Never before had I had dealings with an editor who cared what my opinion on the process was, let alone asked for it!

First things first. Ask to have a contract sent to you as soon as possible. This document concerns the royalties you will receive on book sales, the number of free copies you will be entitled to, the terms of payment, and so on. More and more publishers try to get away with giving first-time authors lousy contracts, so don't just sign on the dotted line without a moment's hesitation. It is worth doing a bit of homework to make sure you are not being sold down the Swanee River!

A literary agent will evaluate a contract for you, but will also take away at least 10% of your royalties for doing so. 10% may not amount to very much at the end of the day when it is from a poetry collection, but it is still 10% of your blood, sweat and tears!

If you are about to become a published author, the chances are that the Society of Authors will accept you as a candidate for membership. The Society exists first and foremost to provide moral support for writers; it also offers legal advice and has established a pension scheme for members. The Society will evaluate any publishing contract free of charge for one of its members, a very valuable service indeed.

The alternatives

If you are told no by publishers again and again and again, what do you do? Other independent people respond to your poetry and it has been accepted in plenty of outlets, but no house will take you on. Perhaps your poetry is not viewed as being 'commercially viable' enough in an age when saleability counts for everything. The answer is not to throw your pen away and abandon all hope; here are the alternatives which are open to you – give them careful thought.

'More and more publishers try to get away with giving first-time authors lousy contracts, so don't just sign on the dotted line without a moment's hesitation. It is worth doing a bit of homework to make sure you are not being sold down the Swanee River!'

44

Self-publishing

This is an option that more and more writers are choosing as production costs decrease all the time and technological wizardry increases all the time. But tread warily, there are landmines embedded in this particular bit of ground, and it's not worth getting injured.

I myself have never self-published anything, but my father has, so I have had the benefit of some fly-on-the-wall observation. The most significant advantage for writers who decide to opt for self-publishing is that after costs have been met, the profits are all their own. The author who chooses to be conventional and to find a publisher in the usual way will be grateful to receive 10% of the sale price of the book once it is in the shops; in my case that amounts to 50p a copy most of the time. The author who chooses to self-publish his or her work may have a return of £3 per copy on a book which retails at a fiver.

But here is the thing to remember, as well as losing the publisher you are also losing the benefits of the publisher. The self-publishing author's two greatest enemies are marketing and distribution, and both are hard nuts to crack unless you are prepared to invest a great deal of time and energy.

You need to work out all your target outlets beforehand, undertake as much homework as you can, to ensure that at the very worst you can recover your expenditure. And in working out your expenditure, you must be certain you are not skimping on vital elements like cover design and quality, which are so important when it comes to 'hooking' a potential buyer. It is also imperative that the finished book is attractive enough to attract the likes of Waterstone's, who will be naturally wary of a self-published title.

Once again, readings will play an enormous part in ensuring that a self-published collection succeeds. In many ways, a local book that describes the waterfall above the town and the standing stones over the hill will do much better than a rather remote collection of poems about Tibet and the monasteries of Nepal. In the latter example, you are offering something for a literary audience only, and immediately you will find the book appealing to 10% or less of the book-buying public.

'If you are told no by publishers again and again and again, what do you do?'

If you self-publish an attractive little volume of poems which has a familiar local name as a title, and which contains many references to people and landmarks in the surrounding district, you will find that many folk who would never bother with poetry will be intrigued and buy this. I've worked in several bookshops and seen this happening over and over again.

The advantage with this type of publication is that you can invest all your energy in targeting a relatively small part of the country. You can try to persuade all sorts of different outlets to stock your book; for example, if you have three or four poems about the Black Bull pub then get the Black Bull to put a few copies in their window. Local authors are often viewed as celebrities; don't let any opportunity to play on that go by.

'The self-publishing author's two greatest enemies are marketing and distribution, and both are hard nuts to crack unless you are prepared to invest a great deal of time and energy.'

A Perthshire author self-published a work on one of the local glens a year or so back. He invested in a quality cover and the book appeared both in hardback and paperback. He did readings for outdoor groups, schools, libraries and churches and after the book had been in print for a year it had sold over 2,000 copies. That may not sound like many books, but remember that many mainstream publishers will be satisfied if a first time novelist sells half that number of copies – across the whole of Britain! A local audience is the key to a self-publishing author's success or downfall – bear that in mind at all times.

Vanity publishing

When you see adverts like the example overleaf, learn to shudder. If you are tempted to respond, then like Odysseus before the Sirens, tie yourself to the mast and refuse to listen. Vanity publishing will only break your heart – and your bank balance.

All sorts of newspapers and literary journals (sadly) carry adverts akin to the fictional one overleaf. No matter how convincing the wording may be, don't believe the blarney.

A vanity publisher may well demand up to several thousand pounds to produce your book. But no matter what may be promised about marketing and distribution, none of it will happen. Nor will the promised agents get your book into the high street shops, for the simple reason that bookshops can smell vanity publishers a mile away, and very rightly want nothing to do with them.

Vanity publications don't know their art from their elbows. They couldn't care less about the quality of the material they receive, only about the quantity of cheques they manage to get hold of. They may give you a list of the people who started off their writing careers by paying to get their first book published, but these are individuals who succeeded despite the vanity publishers, not because of them.

If you are in doubt as to whether or not the operator is a vanity publisher, remember that no mainstream house ever needs to ask for manuscripts – they arrive of their own accord by the sackful. Nor does any editor in his right mind particularly request poetry and memoirs because he would be able to fill the Albert Hall with them after a week. Vanity publishers mention these two genres very cynically in their adverts because they know all too well how difficult the mainstream market is for both poetry and memoirs, and their gleeful hope is that many disillusioned writers will fall into their clutches. And they do, year after year.

I understand how tempting it can be. For several years I was simply desperate to see a first poetry collection in print and I was enraged and grief-stricken every time that precious package of poems came back through the letter-box. I often saw adverts for vanity publishers and the temptation was huge to call a halt to this dreadful waiting and invest my savings in a secret deal. I'm mightily glad that I didn't.

A vanity publication may well come back to haunt you, become a Banquo's ghost you can't get rid of. If the next book you get published is by a mainstream outlet, all sorts of embarrassing and awkward questions may be asked by reviewers and newspaper editors about 'your first book.' Is it worth shelling out three or four figures for a publication which will sell perhaps 50 or a 100 copies?

If you believe your work is good, that you have something to say, and that others believe that too, then don't sign in blood the vanity publisher's contract. Keep on fighting to find a reputable outlet, no matter how small it may be, because at the end of the day you will always know your poetry was published because of its merit, not because of your ability to pay.

'If you are in doubt as to whether or not the operator is a vanity publisher, remember that no mainstream house ever needs to ask for manuscripts – they arrive of their own accord by the sackful.'

MP
MIRANDA PUBLISHING
NEW YORK · LONDON · SYDNEY

Seeks manuscripts of all types for publications.
Memoirs and poetry particularly valued.
Growing publisher with world-wide links.
No material not considered.

The small presses

Another possible publication opportunity lies with the small publishers. There are literally hundreds of such outlets across Britain, often run by individuals already producing small magazines. These are the dedicated soldiers of the poetry world, who work away in lonely, damp attics producing a print-run of a collection of some up-and-coming poet's work.

In many ways it will be easier to have a collection accepted by such an outlet, especially if your work is already known to the editor or has appeared in their magazine. There's no reason why a collection produced in this way shouldn't sell a few hundred copies over time, depending of course on how many readings you can undertake and how much work you can do to publicise the book.

Bear in mind that very few collections of this type will ever end up in shops, except local ones that may be particularly keen to support your writing. I find it very hard to envisage one of the high street chains – even a local branch – taking on a small press publication. Productions will be rarely of a high enough standard to entice them.

Most of the truly small presses will not possess the necessary finance to justify expenditure on marketing and distribution. It will almost certainly be up to you to persuade local libraries and shops to invest in a few copies. I've had to do it myself; apologetically creep into managers' offices, cap in hand, while they moodily scour the pages of my precious work. In time you learn to be bolder, to give as good as you often get.

The terms a small press offers may also be pretty depressing, another reason for negative reactions from the likes of Blackwells and Waterstone's. The high street bookshops often expect 50% of the retail price, something which even mainstream publishers of poetry books find hard to swallow. Such terms would be impossible for the average small publisher, struggling to recoup production and limited distribution costs.

It's very likely, too, that a small press publisher will not offer royalties; indeed there will be no formal contract to start with. It might well be that in the wake of publication you receive 20 or 30 copies of the print-run in lieu of royalties, and that subsidiary copies will be available to you at a reasonable, discounted price.

All this may sound bleak, but it is the hard reality of small press publishing for both poet and producer. Small press publication does, however, remain an invaluable stepping stone for a new writer onto the first rung of the ladder – a move up towards that moment when a mainstream house finally finds the courage to say yes to your collection.

However you get that first collection published, you must be prepared to push and push again at that huge wooden door which stands in front of most new writers. I know a number of poets who have given up disillusioned, having felt in the end the effort required to succeed was just too much. I suppose it is to some extent a question of an individual's reservoir of self-determination and tenacity how they respond to bad reviews and poor sales. I'm not about to throw any stones at writers for giving up in despair, but it is sad to see talented authors throwing away their swords just when it looked as though the battle was turning in their favour.

One useful trick is to keep a folder of praise mail, something I've done since I started out. Put into this the positive letters from publishers, the personal letters of praise you've received from audience members at readings, or from friends who have truly felt inspired by your writing. When the dragons of despair start to burn away your self-confidence, reach for this praise mail and read it until you can get up again onto your literary feet to fight another day.

My story

In 1993 I was in the depths of despair about my own poetry. I'd had work published in many well-known journals both in Britain and overseas, and I knew I wasn't kidding myself that plenty of folk appreciated what I was writing. But my poetry was rural-based, idealistic and rich in imagery. The big publishers wanted different material, and were busy publishing it. In despair I turned to the National Poetry Foundation, and through this organisation came to see my first collection published.

The NPF was a national charity, and membership cost somewhere in the region of £20 per year. After this fee had been paid, members could submit batches of poems to Johnathon Clifford, co-founder of the Foundation, for his evaluation. A maximum of five poems could be contained in each batch, and poems were either accepted or rejected in the same way in which a journal

'Small press publication does, however, remain an invaluable stepping stone for a new writer onto the first rung of the ladder – a move up towards that moment when a mainstream house finally finds the courage to say yes to your collection.'

would operate. Once 40 poems or so had been deemed to be of sufficient merit for publication, the NPF would bring out these pieces in a book at no further expense to the poet. This scheme was made possible by the very generous donations of funds to the NPF by one lady in particular, Rosemary Arthur.

These books would not sell in great quantities. The NPF did not possess the resources or the manpower to distribute its titles widely, so the onus was on the poets themselves to market their collections as effectively as possible. This meant that poets had to be prepared to start reading their work. Not that the NPF would put pressure on their poets to produce sales figures at the end of the year, not at all. But it was only sensible to do all you could to see your collection going out to people if you had fought long and hard for publication!

Johnathon was also very generous about the number of copies of any new collection that he sent out for review. The books themselves were A5 in size with fully laminated illustrated covers. Johnathon discussed at length both front cover illustrations and the content of the back cover blurb with poets, and overall I was most satisfied with the look of our first published collection *Remembering Peter*.

The important thing about an NPF publication was that it provided an up-and-coming poet with a first real stepping stone towards recognition. It would not bring fame, but it would bring fresh hope. It would bring reviews, a bigger audience and the prospect of a mainstream publisher saying yes next time that bit more likely.

Following the death of Rosemary Arthur, the NPF closed in 2002.

Johnathon Clifford

For the past 20 years, Johnathon Clifford has been instrumental in closing down the worst vanity publishers in the UK, and has saved or retrieved in excess of £25 million for authors worldwide. Johnathon is nationally recognised as the person to turn to when it comes to putting a stop to vanity publishers. In recognition for his hard work, Johnathon was presented in 2002 with the Daily Mirror Award, 'The Good Service Award'.

Johnathon runs Vanity Publishing Info, a website for writers (see www.vanitypublishing.info) which has been archived by the British Library for future researchers.

This comprehensive website is packed with information and free publishing advice for aspiring and established authors alike. Johnathon also produces a free advice pack for those looking for a publisher, those seeking self-publishing and those experiencing difficulties with a publisher. The advice pack can be downloaded for free.

Below is an excerpt from Johnathon's advice pack.

A good vanity publisher will not...

- Tell you how well written your book is.

He will discuss with you the true market potential of what you have written and how you can best present your book to the public. He will explain about such things as the function and use of an ISBN number and bar code, and the need for your book (if it is to go on general sale) to be shelf-friendly in appearance.

- Tell you how much better his services are than his competitors and swamp you with reams of review cuttings of other books he's published.

He will simply tell you what services he offers. Bear in mind that although it is important to send out review copies, they normally do not sell books in any significant numbers. Your publisher should, either himself or through an agent, be sending copies of covers (in the first instance) to book buyers and library suppliers well in advance of your publication date.

- Tell you he offers a 'subsidy' or 'co-partnership' or 'joint-venture' publishing service; or any other term that implies he provides a financial commitment of his own to your book – none do.

All vanity publishers are in the business of making money, they are not philanthropic nor will a genuine one try to give you the false impression that he is.

- Tell you that their way is the only way for you to be published and that this or that author in the past had to pay to see his work in print.

Need2Know

They did pay to see their work in print, but not as one of today's vanity publishers would have you do.

- Tell you that, because your work has been accepted on merit, it is to appear in an anthology, then offer to sell you a copy (which he says you don't have to buy) at a 'special discount price.'

He will give you a fee to publish your poem, or offer you a free copy of the anthology, or both.

- Tell you that their anthology is to appear in libraries, and will be on sale in bookshops, when it is read – almost without exception – only by those who appear in it and their families.

- (In the UK) Tell you that he registers your book with Nielsen and also sends a copy of your book to the British Library and (a list of) various universities, as though this is a service for which you should be grateful.

Publishers have to register every book published in the UK with Nielsen, and also have to send one copy to the British Library and five copies to the Legal Deposit Library in Edinburgh, which distributes them to the major universities in England, Wales, Scotland and Northern Ireland.

- Offer to publish 'as many copies as the market demands' or 'x number of copies' while you receive only a few 'free' copies.

A good vanity publisher will agree to publish a fixed number of copies for you at a fixed price, and will explain to you that once you've had your manuscript typeset and good quality plates made, you can always have more copies if necessary after your first run – have too many as that first run and your grandchildren will still be trying to get rid of them from your loft 10 years after you're dead!

- Tell you what a wonderful marketing department he has and that because of their hard work you will recoup your large outlay through its royalties, which are 'higher than anyone else will offer you' and then give you a breakdown of how those royalties work and what they are likely to be. This usually makes little sense – even to a highly trained Accountant.

A good vanity publisher will make sure you understand that the chances of recovering anything other than a very small part of your initial outlay is very negligible as the marketing possibilities for a book by an unknown author are invariably poor and very seldom amount to much more than a launch and promotional follow-up in your own locality.

© Johnathon Clifford, www.vanitypublishing.info.

Summing Up

▪ Don't despair if your collection is not accepted first time around. Keep pushing and have patience.

▪ If you are accepted first time, enjoy the moment to the full!

▪ Once you are accepted, it can be easy to sit back – but you need to ensure you keep track of where your work is and don't let the publisher make all the decisions without you.

▪ Ask for a contract immediately. Check through it carefully, looking out particularly for royalty rates, payment terms and number of free copies. If in doubt, check it with the Society of Authors.

▪ There are other publishing routes you can look at, including self-publishing. However, make sure you do your research before you make any decisions.

▪ Keep a file of your 'praise' mail – use it to keep up your self-confidence.

Chapter Six
Marketing

Signings

I was asked to do a book signing in one of the main high street bookshops in my local town. It was a week before Christmas and the streets were full to capacity with everyone from the tots to the totterers buying gifts for their nearest and dearest. I reckoned on a fairly good avalanche of books; after all, this was my home territory and the world and his donkey was in town.

I didn't sell one book, not a solitary copy. Mind you, neither did Edwina Currie, I'm glad to say, when she came to do a signing in Edinburgh, and I'm sure the bookshop concerned did an awful lot more in the way of advertising beforehand.

I think book signings are best kept local. If you are sitting behind 60 copies of your collection in Waterstone's, you will almost certainly intimidate people. They will be reluctant to pick up a copy of the book from the table because they feel they will be duty-bound to buy it. Local people will know you and probably like you, even if they don't particularly like poetry or know your work. You will be something of a rare species among them, and though they may gently mock you to your face, they will probably praise you behind your back. So sign locally, until genuine fame gives you sufficient confidence to take on the towns.

Advertise beforehand, advertise for all you are worth. Get an interview onto local radio, put a piece into your community magazine, write a press release for your local paper, contact relevant local groups (schools, writers' groups, community centres) and create your own posters if the shop or library giving

'Advertise beforehand, advertise for all you are worth. Get an interview onto local radio, put a piece into your community magazine, and create your own posters if the shop or library giving you the signing will not do so themselves.'

you the signing will not do so themselves. Best of all, tell people the event is taking place. Jungle drums are still the most effective means of communicating in a local community, whether that community be Kentish Town or Carluke.

Make every effort to be friendly to your customers, not just because it is good to be so, but because they may ask you to do a reading in their town hall at Easter or consider talking to the Women's Guild in November. It's all about little acorns making oak trees, and very few contacts or offers should be considered beneath your dignity.

Local radio

I've already mentioned this as an important outlet for writers fighting for a platform and for publicity, whether for a reading you are organising or for promoting your book once published.

I used to think that five men and a sheepdog listened to my local radio station, but I've often been suitably chastened after walking down the high street on the morning following an interview to be told by several passers-by that they'd heard me the night before.

More people listen than you imagine. Your book sales will not go up by hundreds, but recognition of your work certainly will. As soon as you can, contact your local radio and send them a press release and a copy of your new book.

Of course the first time you go into the studio is nerve-racking. Here are some tips for making the experience go smoothly:

- It pays to do a bit of homework beforehand; check with the interviewer, if you can, what sort of framework the interview will have.

- There's no need to prepare a set of written answers to the questions that may come your way, but it will most likely put you at your ease if you have spent a little time thinking about what you want to say in advance.

- Be sure to tell the interviewer the sort of questions you would like to be 'fed' beforehand if that is particularly important, especially if you are in the studio to advertise a reading, a signing or the publication of a book.

- If this is the case, it is no bad thing to write down the relevant details on a piece of paper so the interviewer can make mention of them accurately on air.

- Try to get the chance to read from your own work on radio. It's good practice and poems read aloud often have a power of their own. My own feeling is that a particularly evocative and lyrical poem published in a book is not unlike a butterfly pinned to a board: it requires the poet's voice to release it and breathe life back into its wings.

If you simply cannot bring yourself to conquer the fear of doing a broadcast, or if you have tried and the result was too horrible to remember, then do not despair. But do contact your local radio when you have information regarding your readings or signings or successes; the station will have a news desk and you never know how many people may hear and take note.

Build and maintain a relationship with your contacts at your local radio station – when you have a new publication, send them a copy as soon as possible, and keep them up to date with relevant news and events relating to your work.

Local papers

When considering truly local advertising for your writing, never forget all the newsletters and local rags – which will reach a surprising number of people before they end up in the recycling bin. Just that one weekly paper which lies on the table in the doctor's surgery may be scanned by a hundred or more people.

- Make a list of these outlets and find out the names of editors or staff wherever possible.

- Call them up, or drop them a line, outlining your success and asking them if they would consider covering the story. If so, send a copy of your book if you're promoting a new publication.

- There's little point doing all at once; perhaps have a reading written up in one paper, and a visit to a school covered somewhere else.

- It's particularly important with papers of any real size and influence to read a copy of what they are planning to say about you before it is published. Journalists have a nasty habit of not being able to read their own shorthand,

and I have suffered all too often from book titles being confused, publishers being misspelt, and my own name mangled beyond recognition. It takes just thirty seconds to scan a few paragraphs of prose, and it's worth doing.

- ▦ Cut out and keep pieces that are written about your work, not just for the sake of pride, but because it may prove useful one day. There may come a time when you are asked for quotes about your writing, or when a publisher wants copies of articles from past days.

- ▦ Again, let these outlets know ahead of time when you are to do a signing or reading locally.

- ▦ Find out the best contacts and make sure they learn your name. Sweeten them up and they can become very useful indeed!

Reviews

'At the end of the day, reviews do not sell books, but they do sell poets.'

Everyone wants to be reviewed when they first get a book in print, often because they believe sales will be increased dramatically by coverage.

In actual fact, I don't believe sales are that affected by reviews, either bad or good. Most published poets I know are fairly nonchalant about the effect of reviews; they usually reckon that word of mouth is a more important factor in selling books by far.

But there's no doubt that it is of importance to be seen to be reviewed. I have waxed lyrical about getting your name known as a poet, and here is a vital area for doing just that.

I remember how frustrated I was after my first poetry collection was published, because I expected the reviews to appear like dew after nightfall and there was nothing. I started off sad, became angry and eventually began to fight to get editors to take notice of the book.

In my experience, that has always been the best way to ensure that reviews appear. Make a careful list of all the literary outlets, local papers, radio stations and the like which you reckon might have an interest in your book. Try to get your publisher to send off review copies if you can, but face being told to do this yourself if the publisher is small.

At any rate, try to get review copies from the publisher free of charge. Drop each outlet a line introducing yourself and saying a few words about your book, requesting that you would be very grateful if they reviewed your work. Some you will never hear from again, others are almost certain to follow-up your approach. In all honesty, the better you have done your homework, the more success you are likely to have.

It goes without saying that you should target the more relevant and significant poetry journals. If your collection comprises nature poems, then magazines that focus on these specific themes should be at the top of your list to receive review copies. If the book is about inner-city deprivation and life on a council estate, then target outlets you know favour writing with an urban conscience. Think hard about where your work is going to be best received. It's better to send out two review copies and get two reviews than to send out 20 and get none.

Is a bad review damaging, or is, as they say, all publicity good publicity? I'm not sure. At the end of the day, reviews do not sell books, but they do sell poets. A dreadful review in a prominent journal may wound you and your reputation, but buyers of poetry books will make up their own minds. They may well buy the collection, however bad the reviews, just to see whether those reviews were right or not.

There is no doubt a good review will do you, and your morale, good. To be given recognition, even muted praise, when you are struggling to get a foothold in the poetry world means a great deal indeed. It is formal recognition of your own ability.

So keep these good reviews for the dark days when your poetry thuds down on the mat rejected. They will help convince you it's worth carrying on, that you have what it takes.

Readings

Once you have a book in print, if not long before, you will be undertaking readings. Try to be as imaginative as possible with these, especially in a local context, because the scope is endless. You will find that women's guilds, retirement groups, youth clubs and church societies can all prove interested audiences. Obviously you must be careful to tailor your reading according to the needs of each group; never become cocky and begin 'recycling' talks. Treat every reading as unique and every person in your audience as an individual; this is no more than you would want or expect if you were one of the audience.

Reading in schools

When you have plenty of courage and a good deal of experience, think about undertaking a school reading. Your local authority will be able to give you leads on likely schools, and letters of approach to head teachers are advisable.

Bear in mind that staff are vigilant about visitors and may want to know more of your background before extending an invitation. My advice is to begin at the top and work your way down. It's easiest to make headway with the oldest pupils, who are likely to be less cynical and more mature. I prefer to speak to a group of youngsters who have opted to come to listen, and not been coerced; a compulsory event will not make your task any the easier.

'When you have plenty of courage and a good deal of experience, think about undertaking a school reading.'

What do you cover with them? It's simpler for me because I am a writer of novels and children's fiction as well as poetry, but there is plenty of scope for discussion and tuition within poetry alone.

- Ask the teacher before you visit the school how you can most assist. Generally I offer to read some pupils' work beforehand, something that is almost always welcomed by the teaching staff and the young writers alike.

- Think about the story areas of their writing, and start your talk by praising the scope of their imagination, the use of imagery, the bravery of their choice of topics, etc.

- Then talk about where they might be able to strengthen their poetry, always doing so constructively, without making them feel you have all the answers. Good poetry is in the eye of the beholder; no matter how long our apprenticeship we must not become arrogant as poets.

- Try at all times to get them to start talking about and discussing the components of good writing among themselves. (This generally will be made a lot easier if the class teacher is not present to intimidate them, but that is not always possible.)

- Try to pass on to them something of your enthusiasm for this strange and wonderful poetry-writing life. That is a great privilege.

Reading in prisons

Conducting readings and workshops in prison is not dissimilar, nor is it much more daunting than facing 25 bored teenagers.

Going in the gates is of course a trial – if you'll excuse the pun – and the prison environment is challenging to come to terms with. The first time I undertook a workshop in prison I came into the designated room with jelly legs and swam through a blue sea of cigarette smoke to a vacant chair. 'I'm very glad to be here,' I said, making my usual opening remark. 'Well, speak for yourself!' came the quick-witted response from the back.

I think it is even more important in this context that you speak to an audience that has chosen to listen, and not been forced at the point of a bayonet. Creative writing is of real importance to prisoners all over the country, and if you visit to offer insight and advice to a writing group, you will be given a real welcome.

Go into prison as yourself. Don't try to be 'one of them', having formed a false stereotype beforehand of the 'average prisoner'. You'll find prisoners from every class and every walk of life inside. Be yourself, because they will respect that, whatever your background.

I went in trying hard to be long-haired and ordinary; in two minutes they had me sussed out – someone asked which public school I'd been to.

'Treat every reading as unique and every person in your audience as an individual; this is no more than you would want or expect if you were one of the audience.'

Finances

A note on finances. Do bear these points in mind when planning readings and workshops for the above groups:

- Visits to schools and prisons generally receive support from the local authority.

- Don't be shy to ask about this payment; the labourer is worthy of their hire.

- A fee should be payable, in addition to travelling expenses.

Workshops

Workshops for up-and-coming writers can be daunting; I say this from past experience.

There is a vast amount of difference between a reading and a workshop. The first you can undertake whenever you feel you have the confidence to share a stage with other poets, or even to go solo. Workshops are much harder work. They require a confidence in your own writing ability and style, a knowledge of how to craft good poetry and hone it effectively, an ability to lead and steer a writing group in a set direction.

Given the choice between a reading and a workshop, I'd plump for the former every time. But a good workshop can be rewarding and challenging all the same, it depends to a certain extent on the group. It's inadvisable to visit the Feminist Writing Tigresses of Upper Teesdale as a first venture.

People are realising more and more the value of poetry and creative writing in general as far as therapy is concerned, and many groups have been started in recent years to encourage those with troubled pasts. The Survivors' Poetry Network, for example, exists to provide both a support and a creative inspiration for people who are survivors, in any sense at all, of mental health problems. Such groups are keen to invite along practising poets to pass on advice and encouragement to members, and often the chance to offer constructive criticism of members' work.

Adult education groups are another possible starting point for workshops, or even children's classes if you have experience with that age group from before and have the ability to fire young minds.

Whatever the starting point and however much experience you gain, workshops remain hard work. No two groups are ever the same, so you should never become complacent and begin trying to cut corners by 'recycling' programmes.

Prepare as much as you can beforehand, while still being flexible enough to change tack in the course of a workshop if that seems right. Always have more material than you need rather than too little; listen to other leaders of workshops and learn from both what they do well and what they do badly.

Most of all, enjoy every minute of what you do. You are passing on your love of creativity and poetry, and the more you do of that, the more your audience – whoever they are – will respond. Poetry is about life itself – live both to the full!

Social media

Using online social media as a marketing tool is becoming really popular, and can be used to help make a 'noise' about your publication or latest poetry reading or signing. If you keep your updates interesting and of value to your readers, you will soon build up a following to 'spread the word', and can meet other poets along the way. Here are some suggested social networking tools for you to try:

- Facebook: set up a personal account promoting your profile as a poet. You could even set up a 'facebook page' to promote poetry readings, your latest publication, or other literary events you are organising or attending. It can also be used to make contact with other writers. Visit www.facebook.com for further information.

- Linked In: this social networking site will allow you to create a profile to connect with other professionals. It's rather like a 'professional' version of facebook. Visit www.linkedin.com for further information.

- Twitter: this allows you to create a profile and send out short messages (rather like the status tool on facebook). People can choose to follow your 'tweets', and you can follow others'. Using twitter and facebook, you can search for poetry magazines, journals, publishers and other writing communities that have online profiles, which would be a handy way of keeping up to date with the latest news and submissions. Visit www.twitter.com to get started.

- Blogs: set up a blog and start updating the world about your poetry events and publications. You can get some ideas from www.blogger.com or www.wordpress.org.

- Website: you could set up your own website to market and sell yourself.

'You are passing on your love of creativity and poetry, and the more you do of that, the more your audience – whoever they are – will respond. Poetry is about life itself – live both to the full!'

This could be as budget-friendly or expensive as you desire – from a basic website that promotes yourself as a poet, to a more technical one that allows you to sell your publications.

- Emails: if you do join a social networking site or create a website or blog, be sure to include the links to these in your email signature, and start generating a following.

Summing Up

- You need to spread the word about your work. Book signings are an important start, but you need to keep them local and advertise beforehand. Target your local radio stations, local paper and local magazines.

- Try to get reviews of your work in as many outlets as possible – from local media to relevant national magazines and outlets. Reviews save you spending money on expensive adverts.

- Once your work is in print you need to start doing readings and workshops. Remember to always tailor to your audience.

- Readings – think outside the box for publicity.

- As explained earlier, you will be expected to do a vast majority of the publishing yourself. However, if you've had a book published, your publisher may be able to help. If this is the case, make sure you keep in contact with them – there's no point overlapping in your efforts.

Chapter Seven

A Checklist for Poets

Magazines and journals

Here is a representative selection of well-established poetry magazines and journals.

10th Muse

33 Hartington Road, Southampton, SO14 0EW
www.nonism.org.uk/muse
An occasional publication. No payment for publication. Publishes poetry, reviews, short prose and graphics. Contributors receive a free copy of the magazine.

Acumen

Patricia Oxley (general editor), 6 The Mount, Higher Furzeham, Brixham, South Devon, TQ5 8QY
www.acumen-poetry.co.uk
Three issues a year. A very beautiful journal, as likely to accept the work of an unknown as that of the Poet Laureate. Short poems will always succeed best here because of the pressure on space. Always responds to submissions quickly and individually. Small payment, if any, for published poems.

Agenda

The Editor, The Wheelwrights, Fletching Street, Mayfield, East Sussex, TN20 6TL
www.agendapoetry.co.uk
Agenda is a respected poetry journal. Publishes a selection of poetry, critical essays and reviews. Also runs an initiative for young poets – see 'Online Broadsheets.' Looks for poems that are 'deeply felt and well crafted' and regularly publishes new work.

Ambit

17 Priory Gardens, London, N6 5QY
www.ambitmagazine.co.uk
Quarterly. Promotes new writers and new writing. Token payment for writers as it's a non-profit making magazine, but a free copy of the issue your work appears in will be sent. Prints original poetry, short fiction, art and reviews. Visit the website for submission information and guidance.

Candelabrum Poetry Magazine

Published twice yearly. Has subscribers from all around the world. You can read more about this at www.poetrymagazines.org.uk.

Chapman

4 Broughton Place, Edinburgh, EH1 3RX
www.chapman-pub.co.uk
Focuses on Scottish writing but many issues are concerned with wider themes: women's poetry, cultural politics, etc. Poems, short stories, articles and reviews. Payment made for published poems. Focus is Scotland, but also publishes literature by non-Scots and in translation from other languages.

The Countryman

The Water Mill, Broughton Hall, Skipton, North Yorkshire, BD23 3AG
www.countrymanmagazine.co.uk
Monthly magazine. Poems are used as 'fillers' to follow articles and to enhance photography. All the poems used have an outdoor theme, from harvesting to hearing the first cuckoo of spring. A natural outlet for poets concentrating on rural topics. Payment made for published poems.

Cutting Teeth

Cutting Teeth, The Arts and Cultural Development Office, 17A Castlemilk Arcade, Glasgow, G45 9AA
This literature magazine comprises of new writing by a mixture of well established and previously unpublished writers.

Envoi

Meirion House, Glan yr afon, Tanygrisiau, Blaenau Ffestiniog,
Gwynedd, LL41 3SU
www.cinnamonpress.com/envoi
Published by Cinnamon Press as a journal. Three issues a year. Contains the
poetry of both established and new writers. No particular style favoured, but
it would seem gentler and more traditional writing is better liked than the in-
your-face poetry of the ultra brash. The editor likes to print a number of poems
from each author, so work hard to make a submission count. No payment for
published poems. Poets from Wales, the UK and world welcome.

Krax

63 Dixon Lane, Leeds, LS12 4RR
Krax is an A5, card covered publication, containing poems, short stories, an
interview, illustrations and a pull-out reviews section. There is no editorial. The
poetry tends towards the funny with lots of puns and clever word play and
including a number of limericks.

Magma

23 Pine Walk, Carshalton, SM5 4ES
www.magmapoetry.com
Three issues a year. Publishes contemporary poetry, with a different editor
for every issue. Submission rules online. Welcomes unknown, emerging and
established poets.

New Welsh Review

PO Box 170, Aberystwyth, Ceredigion, SY23 1WZ
www.newwelshreview.com
Quarterly. Focuses on Welsh writing but outsiders are definitely welcome.
Poems, short stories, articles, interviews and reviews. Fairly generous payment
made for published poems. Magazine is a platform for debate, describes itself
as 'dynamic, curious, lively and outward-looking.'

New Writing Scotland

www.arts.gla.ac.uk/scotlit/asls
ASLS, Department of Scottish Literature, 7 University Gardens, University of Glasgow, Glasgow, G12 8QH
An annual volume publishing poetry and prose from both new and established writers. Every piece appears in print for the first time. Writers can be living in Scotland, or 'Scots by birth, upbringing or inclination'.

Orbis

Carole Baldock (editor), 17 Greenhow Avenue, West Kirby, Wirral, Cheshire, CH48 5EL.
Quarterly. Very open to poetry by new writers. Includes the work of a feature poet in each issue. Orbis is very well known; be patient when waiting for news of your submission. Small payment made for published poems. More information can be found at www.poetrymagazines.org.uk.

Other Poetry

Fourlawshill Top, Bellingham, Hexham, Northumberland, NE48 2EY
www.otherpoetry.com
'Dedicated to good poetry in all its forms.' Welcomes submissions of poetry all year round, no restrictions on subject matter, theme, length or style. Submission details on the website.

Poetry London

Colette Bryce (poetry editor), 81 Lambeth Walk, London, SE11 6DX
www.poetrylondon.co.uk
Published three times a year. National and international poetry magazine. Publishes work from established and unpublished writers from across the UK and worldwide. A third of the pages are devoted to poets who have not yet published their first collection.

Poetry Review

www.poetrysociety.org.uk
Click on the 'poetry review' tab for details. *Poetry Review* is the Poetry Society's internationally acclaimed poetry magazine, published quarterly and sent to every full member of the Poetry Society. Submission information is on the website.

Poetry Scotland

Sally Evans (editor), 91-93 Main Street, Callander, FK17 8BQ.
www.poetryscotland.co.uk
Broadsheet magazine. Open to all poets from the UK, although Scottish writing is the main focus.

Poetry Wales

57 Nolton Street, Bridgend, CF31 3AE
www.poetrywales.co.uk
Quarterly magazine with an international reputation for excellent poems, features and reviews from Wales and beyond. Details of how to submit poems on the website – with a different address for submissions.

The Rialto

The Editor, The Rialto, PO Box 309, Aylsham, Norwich, NR11 6LN
www.therialto.co.uk
Independent poetry magazine and award winning poetry publisher. Three issues a year. Receives support from the Arts Council. Features international names and established poets alongside new poets.

Smiths Knoll

The Editors, Goldings, Goldings Lane, Leiston, Suffolk, IP16 4EB
www.smithsknoll.co.uk
A leading poetry magazine of new poetry. 60 pages – no more than one poem per page. Swift response to subscribers. Responds to submissions within a fortnight. Runs a workshop weekend and mentoring scheme.

Stand

School of English, Leeds University, Leeds, LS2 9JT
www.people.vcu.edu/~dlatane/stand-maga
Quarterly literary magazine. Only considers previously unpublished material and pays on publication – see website for submission guidelines. Features new writing, poetry, fiction and criticism. The magazine works in close association with the School of English at the University of Leeds.

Staple

Wayne Burrows (editor), 114-116 St Stephen's Road, Sneinton, Nottingham, NG2 4JS

www.staplemagazine.co.uk

Three issues a year. Supports both established and up-and-coming poets. Also welcomes short fiction, articles and reviews. Allow up to two months for a response. Looks for 'fresh approaches to writing.' Small payment made for published poems.

Weyfarers

1 Mountside, Guildford, Surrey, GU2 4JD

www.weyfarers.com

Weyfarers publishes modern and traditional poetry and accepts work from both new and established poets from the UK and all parts of the world. Publishes three times a year.

Online magazines and journals

Dragon Heart Press

www.dragonheartpress.com

Dragon Heart is a digital publisher of poetry in the UK. Submissions welcomed – details online. Details of competitions on website.

Free Verse: A Journal of Contemporary Poetry and Poetics

http://english.chass.ncsu.edu/freeverse

Bi-annual electronic journal publishing free verse. Published US work but also invites English language submissions from outside America. Submission information on the website.

Glasgow Review

www.glasgowreview.co.uk

Publishes poetry, art, articles, short stories. Submission information online.

Osprey Journal

www.ospreyjournal.co.uk
Scotland's international journal of literature, arts and ideas. This online journal publishes poetry, short stories, art, reviews and articles.

Pens on Fire

www.pensonfire.com
Online magazine for short fiction and poetry. Guidelines for submission on the website. Helps give many writers their first by-line.

Poetry Monthly

www.poetrymonthly.com
Published 1st of each month. The magazine is a free pdf file. Submission information on the website.

For a comprehensive list of current poetry magazines and online emagazines, a checklist is produced by the Poetry Library in London. Here you will also find up-to-date information on poetry competitions and festivals. Visit www. poetrylibrary.org.uk. You will also find extensive lists in the *Writers' and Artists' Yearbook* – visit www.writersandartists.co.uk for details.

Publishers

For mainstream publishers of poetry, I think the best information is to be had from the *Poetry Writers' Yearbook*, and the *Writers' and Artists' Yearbook*. A regularly updated list is also available from the Poetry Library, which splits publishers into three types: major book publishers, small book publishers and ebook publishing.

If you want to browse through the productions of the leading publishers, then spend a morning in Waterstone's or find a specialist poetry bookshop.

For small press publishers turn to *The Writer's Handbook* (see www.thewritershandbook.com). Here you will find enough to keep you happy for many moons; the only problem is it's virtually impossible to see the wood for the trees.

The following list comprises reputable, middle-sized presses which may provide that vital stepping stone to a contract with a mainstream publisher. Details are correct at the time of going to press, but it is always worthwhile checking details on the Internet.

Cinnamon Press

Meirion House, Glan yr afon, Tanygrisiau, Blaenau Ffestiniog, Gwynedd, LL41 3SU
www.cinnamonpress.com

Flambard Press

Holy Jesus Hospital, City Road, Newcastle upon Tyne, NE1 2AS
www.flambardpress.co.uk

The Frogmore Press

21 Mildmay Road, Lewes, East Sussex, BN7 1PJ
www.frogmorepress.co.uk

Headland Publications

York Avenue, West Kirby, Wirral, CH48 3JF
www.headlandpublications.co.uk

Iron Press

5 Marden Terrace, Cullercoats, North Shields, Northumberland, NE30 4PD
www.ironpress.co.uk

Salt Publishing

14a High Street, Fulbourn, Cambridge, CB21 5DH
www.saltpublishing.com

Scottish Cultural Press

Unit 6, Newbattle Abbey Business Park, Newbattle Road, Dalkeith, EH22 3LJ
www.scottishbooks.com

White Leaf Press

PO Box 734, Aylesbury, Bucks, HP20 9AL
www.whiteleafpress.co.uk

The Women's Press

27 Goodge Street, London, W1T 2LD
www.the-womens-press.com

Competitions

The following are but a few of the dozens of poetry competitions run every year in Britain. You will be able to build up a comprehensive list by contacting the Poetry Library and regularly researching on the Internet. Contact individual competitions for entry forms.

- The Arvon International Poetry Competition: www.arvonfoundation.org.
- The Frogmore Poetry Prize: see Frogmore Press contact details opposite.
- The Cardiff International Poetry Competition: www.academi.org/cipc/.
- The National Poetry Competition: www.poetrysociety.org.uk.

Awards and bursaries

Arts Council of England

Awards are made each year to already published writers of poetry, fiction, autobiography or biography. For full details of application procedures contact the Literature Department, Arts Council of England, 14 Great Porter Street, London, SW1P 3NQ, www.artscouncil.org.uk.

Arts Council of Wales Bursaries

Similar awards are made to artists resident in Wales each year. For further details contact the Arts Council of Wales, Bute Place, Cardiff, CF10 5AL, www.artswales.org.uk.

The Booktrust

The Booktrust give away prizes and awards that celebrate work for all ages and categories. The website has details of current competitions and awards. Book Trust, Book House, 45 East Hill, London, SW18 2QZ, www.booktrust.org.uk.

The Brit Writers' Awards

Awards for unpublished writers. Enter poetry, short stories, songs. You could win £10,000 – the largest prize ever offered to unpublished writers in a creative writing competition. See www.britwriters.co.uk.

Creative Scotland

A number of bursaries are awarded to Scottish writers each year. Full details are available from www.creativescotland.com. Click on 'Arts, Screen and Creative Industries', and then 'Literature.'

The Eric Gregory Awards

The most recognised awards for younger poets in Britain; five or six poets are chosen each year. Candidates must be British and under the age of 30 at 31 March in the year the Award is made. A collection of not more than 30 poems must be submitted no later than 31st October to the Society of Authors, 84 Drayton Gardens, London, SW10 9SB. Visit www.societyofauthors.org/eric-gregory for full details and to download an entry form.

Forward Prizes for Poetry

Created to bring contemporary to a larger audience. The awards are for both established and emerging writers. Visit www.forwardartsfoundation.org/poetry.htm.

There are many awards and bursaries 'out there'. It's just a question of searching for what's the best – which is where Internet research comes in. However, one important resource is the *Poetry Writers' Yearbook*, published by A & C Black each year (see book list). This has latest details of competitions, awards and bursaries.

Foreign journals

As I have already made clear in my section on getting poetry published abroad, the market is huge. Detective work to sound out the best outlets is the only solution. Below are some of the journals I have found most helpful and successful, but keep researching for new outlets online.

Australia

Imago

GPO Box 2434, Brisbane 4001 Queensland.
Bi-annually. This A5 glossy paperback is as handsome as a Penguin book. The contents are divided between short stories and poetry, and the last 10 or so pages are devoted to reviews of new Australian publications. But the contributors to *Imago* are a truly international bunch, and there is plenty of scope here for British poets. One of Australia's friendliest outlets. Payment is made for all published work.

Westerly

The Westerly Centre, The University of Western Australia, Crawley, Western Australia 6009.
www.westerlycentre.uwa.edu.au
Bi-annual. This journal has an international reputation and often contains writing by highly respected authors, Australian and non-Australian alike. It has perhaps more of an academic edge than *Imago*, but high quality poems and short stories will always succeed nonetheless. Payment is made for all published work. Visit the website and click on 'Westerly' to be taken to the journal. Submission information on website.

Canada

Queen's Quarterly

144 Barrie Street, Queen's University, Kingston, Ontario, K71 3N6
www.queensu.ca/quarterly
This has to be Canada's finest literary journal. An A5 production, it contains over 200 pages of articles, short stories, interviews, photography and poetry. The editors reply to submissions very quickly, but often poetry is returned simply because they have so much material on their hands. Payment for published poems is very high. Detailed submission information can be found on the website.

South Africa

New Coin

ISEA, Rhodes University, PO Box 94, Grahamstown 6140.
Appears bi-annually and is produced by Rhodes University Press. The journal is A5 in size and contains somewhat over 100 pages of poetry, short fiction and reviews. By far the greatest percentage of work is by African writers, but the editors are very open to writing from abroad. No payment is made for published work. New Coin also has a facebook page; search 'New Coin: South African Poetry.'

Chapter Eight

Afterword

This book is a revised edition of my 1998 publication, *Poetry: How to Get Published, How to Get Paid*. As I look back on these chapters written for the book I realise that in many ways very little has changed when it comes to publishing poetry. It's still just as much as ever about acquiring a reputation in order to get published, and once the book is printed doing the same work to win attention for it in the world.

Sadly, poetry is as little valued by most bookshops as ever. It's even harder to find a volume of poetry in one of the high street bookshop chains – and when you do happen to catch a glimpse of one there, the odds are it'll be an anthology of verse on dogs or cats. The fact is that most publishers of poetry simply can't afford to have their books here; the mark up demanded by the big chains is far too high. Fortunately, that's not the whole story.

The good news is that even in the midst of a hugely challenging economic climate, lots of independent bookstores are appearing around the country. These shops are the friends of local authors (not just poets, but writers of all kinds). I give many readings through independent bookshops; I find out about the book groups that may be run through them; I do my best to support what they're trying to do for and with local schools, community groups and more.

Small, independent bookshops care about local authors and want to know about them and work with them; they're the best place to think of giving a first reading with a few other poet friends. What about even thinking of setting up a tiny festival through the bookstore? Involve the local school, the church, the pub – it's amazing what mighty oaks can grow from the tiniest of acorns.

Spreading the word has become so much easier thanks to the Internet. When a new collection of my work is published, I send out an email to somewhere in the region of 250 friends of my work. Not only do many of these folk order copies for themselves, they also tend to buy for other friends. Because the poetry community is small and scattered, it's hugely important to reach as many as possible with information, and email is the prefect solution.

I have a website too through which I give news of the readings, talks and writing workshops I'm to be running over the next months. I'm not nearly dedicated enough when it comes to the website; some people would be writing a weekly blog for the main page, whereas I manage one every couple of months. Sometimes I despair and think the whole business of having and updating a website is a waste of time; then one morning I switch on the computer to find a message from Germany or America – a reader wanting a signed copy of a book or looking for information on a writing course.

Even now I spend at least an hour a week scouring the net for new leads: publishers, festivals, libraries, events. I look for bookshops running poetry events, schools with a particular bias towards the genre, projects run by councils that might be worth investigating.

I still don't pretend to make my living as a writer from poetry; because I'm on the edge of wild country, I describe myself as a literary crofter. Crofters have to do all manner of different tasks in order to make a semblance of a living: driving a local taxi, selling eggs, planting trees, fishing. Similarly, I write children's books, fiction, magazine articles, and books like this on the whole subject of the creative writing business. But more and more of what I do is connected in some way with poetry, and there's not a shadow of a doubt that having the net has helped enormously in that task. And some people must do far more than me in this respect. I've never really searched for virtual poetry magazines or submitted my work electronically. I still live first and foremost by paper and pen – and I don't ever see that changing.

As I think back to how I started out I realise that one of the great losses is the National Poetry Foundation. When I despaired that having a first collection of work published was going to prove an impossibility, the NPF provided that first platform into print. Not only did it mean the publication of a thin volume of work, it meant as many review copies as I wanted sent out to magazine editors, radio stations and poetry organisations. It also meant learning to work with an editor, and Johnathon Clifford devoted many years of labour to that work and to making the Foundation known. The passing of the organisation is a great loss to poets starting out; I can only hope that a similarly altruistic and generous outfit may take its place in coming years.

Is it any easier to get a first collection published than it was 10 years ago? I think it's probably no easier, but the poetry publishing scene has evolved quite radically – and for the better, I believe. It has to be good that London dominance has diminished; fine-looking collections of work are appearing from every corner of these islands, and it's quite simply no longer the case that all the most highly acclaimed poets are with Faber & Faber. However, some things never change. The place to be a poet and the place to be seen doing poetry is still London town; I suspect that's true whether you want to be a clown or a carpenter too – London is the place to begin, the place to win your reputation.

However, that doesn't mean you have to live there! I grew up on the edge of Highland Scotland and that's where I am to this day. I do try to have the courage to face London twice a year all the same; I set up meetings with publishers and I make contact with venues for readings. I don't do enough, but I do a bit. The fact is that although Manchester and Glasgow and Bristol and a number of other places have become significant for poetry, none has quite the importance of London.

But you don't need to go anywhere near London to find a poetry festival. That's one of the hugely positive developments over the past decade, the establishment of festivals dedicated specifically to poetry – with readings, talks, workshops, poetry walks, children's events, performance poetry, local radio programmes and more. If there's one close to you then work hard knocking at their door; if they won't give you the chance to read, then what about setting up your own event with friends? The opportunity's waiting to be seized; you have devotees of the genre all around you – people who can't have enough poetry! Be creative; think what would work best and do everything in your power to advertise the event effectively.

At the end of the day what hasn't changed one iota is that to break through in this world – like anywhere else – you need energy and commitment and determination. Of course you need some self-belief; you have to feel that what you're writing is worth reading, that you have something to say and that you have developed and found your voice. Sometimes I used to feel that this campaign to break through, to win some kind of name for myself, must be like planning a battle. Every day when the rejection slips arrived I sat down and thought, leafed through my books and worked out how I'd try again. I enjoyed the struggle (you have to, or in the end the stuffing will be knocked out of you).

But first and foremost I come back to this; poems should be a by-product of living. Writing and crafting a poem of which you're proud is something in and of itself; if it happens to be published, that's worth celebrating, but it's the poem and what it stands for that matters more than anything. Do all you can to get published; work as hard as possible to market your book – but don't ever forget to love searching for words: the best words, in the best order.

Help List

Support for writers

Arts Council, England

www.artscouncil.org.uk
Works to get great art to everyone by championing, developing and investing in artistic experiences that enrich people's lives.

Contemporary Writers

www.contemporarywriters.com
This website is great if you want to search for poets to inspire you. Its database contains up-to-date profiles of some of the UK and Commonwealth's most important living writers. Included are writers from the Republic of Ireland the council has worked with. You'll find reviews, bibliographies and biographies – ideal if you're looking for fresh material to read!

Forward Press Ltd

Remus House, Coltsfoot Drive, Peterborough, PE2 9JX
Tel: 01733 890099
info@forwardpress.co.uk
www.forwardpress.co.uk
Forward Press is the largest publisher of new poetry in the world. They hold regular competitions for both adults and young writers, and selected poetry is published in anthologies. Submission themes are regularly updated on the website. Forward Press also has a section specifically for young writers, see www.youngwriters.co.uk.

Irish Writers' Centre

www.writerscentre.ie
Supports established and aspiring writers. Offers workshops, lectures, seminars and courses.

National Association of Writers' Groups (NAWG)

PO Box 3266. Stoke-on-Trent, ST10 9BD
www.nawg.co.uk
The aim of this organisation is to bring writers' groups and individuals together. There is a searchable directory of members across the UK on the website, as well as articles and details of latest competitions and events. Visit the website for contact details.

Northern Poetry Library

Gas House Lane, Morpeth, Northumberland, NE61 1TA
Tel: 01670 500390
www.northumberland.gov.uk
Holds the largest collection of contemporary poetry in England outside of London. You will find anthologies, poetry collections and magazines.

The Poetry Archive

PO Box 286, Stroud, Gloucestershire, GL6 1AL
www.poetryarchive.org
The Poetry Archive exists to help make poetry accessible by all. A comprehensive selection of poetry is online for you to listen to and read. Separate sections also included for teachers and students.

The Poetry Library

www.poetrylibrary.org.uk
www.poetrymagazines.org.uk
The library holds a comprehensive collection of poetry. The website also allows you to find poetry magazines in the UK.

The Poetry Society

www.poetrysoc.com
A charitable organisation providing information for specialists and the general public. Visit the website for details of events, competitions, commissions, promotions, publications. Writers can get help with their poetry here. Home of the *Poetry Review*.

The Poetry Trust

9 New Cut, Halesworth, Suffolk, IP19 8BY
Tel: 01986 835950
www.thepoetrytrust.org
One of the UK's flagship poetry organisations, delivering a year-round live
and digital programme, creative education opportunities, courses, news,
events, prizes and publications.

The Scottish Poetry Library

Tel: 0131 5572876
www.spl.org.uk
The library holds contemporary Scottish poetry, poetry from around the world,
poetry for children, current magazines and back numbers – great if you need
some inspiration! You can also read poetry online.

The Society of Authors

Tel: 0207 3736642
www.societyofauthors.org
The Society of Authors provides information and advice to all writers. Today it
has more than 8,500 members writing in all areas of the profession. Visit the
website for news, events and resources.

Vanity Publishing Info

www.vanitypublishing.info
Run by Johnathon Clifford, this is an invaluable resource providing clear
information about vanity publishing. Free advice pack can be downloaded
from the website.

Writers' Forum

www.writers-forum.com
This is a magazine dedicated to helping new and aspiring writers. Packed with
the latest information, the magazine includes tips and advice from established
writers, as well as experts in the publishing world. It also runs regular poetry
competitions. Visit the website for further information and individual contacts.

Poetry courses

The Arvon Foundation

60 Farringdon Road, London, EC1R 3GA
Tel: 0207 3242554
london@arvonfoundation.org
www.arvonfoundation.org
Offers a wide choice of courses. Use the online search facility to find poetry courses near you. A separate section included for young people. Hosts the Arvon International Poetry Competition.

Course Enquiries - Exeter Phoenix

Bradninch Place, Gandy Street, Exeter, EX4 3LS
Tel: 01392 667081
www.exeterphoenix.org.uk
Click on the 'education' tab for details of courses and workshops.

Directory of Poetry Courses

www.writewords.org.uk
Click on 'directory' and then under poetry, click 'courses.' You can also find groups, competitions, resources, magazines and news.

Literature Training

PO Box 23595, Leith, EH6 7YX
info@literaturetraining.com
www.literaturetraining.com
Click on 'training and events' for details of workshops, courses and conferences being held across the UK by training providers.

The Poetry School

81 Lambeth Walk, London, SE11 6DX
Tel: 0207 5821679
administration@poetryschool.com
www.poetryschool.com

Offers a programme of classes to teach adults to write poetry. You can choose from one day courses, through to one year courses. There are teaching centres across the UK. Online courses are available to download too.

Ty Newydd Writers' Centre

Ty Newydd, Llanystumdwy, Cricieth, Gwynedd, LL52 OLW
Tel: 01766 522811
post@tynewydd.org
www.tynewydd.org
National writers' centre for Wales. List of courses on the website.

University of St Andrews

School of English, Castle House, University of St Andrews, Fife, KY16 9AL
Tel: 01334 462666
english@st-andrews.ac.uk
www.st-andrews.ac.uk

University of Derby

Student Information Centre, Kedleston Road, Derby, DE22 1GB
Tel: 01332 590500
askadmissions@derby.ac.uk
www.derby.ac.uk

University of East Anglia

Continuing Education Admissions Team, University of East Anglia, Norwich, Norfolk, NR4 7JT
Tel: 01603 593252
cce.admiss@uea.ac.uk
www.uea.ac.uk

University of Reading

Centre for Continuing Education, London Road, Reading, Berkshire, RG1 5AQ
Tel: 0118 3782347
continuing-education@reading.ac.uk
www.reading.ac.uk

University of Warwick

Centre for Lifelong Learning, Westwood Campus, University of Warwick, Coventry, CV4 7AL
Tel: 024 76524617
cll@warwick.ac.uk
www2.warwick.ac.uk

This is obviously only a small selection of universities – check your local university or college to see if they run poetry courses.

Poetry magazines & journals

Below are some other suggestions for magazines – again, this is only a small selection. Visit their websites for further information and submission guidelines.

Erbacce

5 Farrell Close, Melling, Liverpool, L31 1BU
www.erbacce.com

The Frogmore Papers

21 Mildmay Road, Lewes, East Sussex, BN7 1PJ
www.frogmorepress.co.uk

The New Writer

PO Box 60, Cranbrook, Kent, TN17 2ZR
www.thenewwriter.com

The North

Submissions Department, The Poetry Business, Bank Street Arts, 32-40 Bank Street, Sheffield, S1 2DS
www.poetrybusiness.co.uk

Poetry Nation Review

4th Floor, Alliance House, 30, Cross Street, Manchester, M2 7AQ
www.pnreview.co.uk

Sentinel Literary Quarterly

Unit 136, 113-115 George Lane, London, E18 1AB
www.sentinelpoetry.org.uk

South Poetry Magazine

PO Box 3744, Cookham, Maidenhead, SL6 9UY
www.southpoetry.org

Stride

Rupert Loydell, submissions@stridemagazine.co.uk
www.stridemagazine.co.uk

The Wolf Magazine

3, Holly Mansions, Fortune Green Road, West Hampstead, London, NW6 1UB
www.wolfmagazine.co.uk

Performance venues for poets

Apple and Snakes

www.applesandsnakes.org

The Poetry Café

poetrycafe@poetrysoc.com
Visit www.poetrysoc.com for further details.

The Poetry Library

www.poetrylibrary.org.uk

Scottish Poetry Library

www.spl.org.uk

All contact details were correct at the time of going to press. However, magazines and journals inevitably change, so you are advised to check details before sending work, and keep looking online for new outlets.

Book List

Book Proposals – The Essential Guide
By Stella Whitelaw, Need2Know, Peterborough, 2011.

Creating Fictional Characters – The Essential Guide
By Jean Saunders, Need2Know, Peterborough, 2011.

Poet's Market
By Robert Lee Brewer, Writer's Digest Books, Cincinnati, 2011.

Poetry Writers' Yearbook
By Gordon Kerr (ed), A & C Black, London, 2008.

Publishing Poetry – The Essential Guide
By Kenneth Steven, Need2Know, Peterborough, 2010.

Writers' and Artists' Yearbook
By A & C Black, London.
www.writersandartists.co.uk.

The Writer's Handbook
By Barry Turner (ed), Macmillan, Hampshire.
www.thewritershandbook.com.

Writing Dialogue – The Essential Guide
By Jean Saunders, Need2Know, Peterborough, 2011.

Writing Non-Fiction Books – The Essential Guide
By Gordon Wells, Need2Know, Peterborough, 2010.

Writing Romantic Fiction – The Essential Guide
By Jean Saunders, Need2Know, Peterborough, 2011.

For *The Writers' Handbook* and the *Writers' and Artists' Yearbook*, try to get hold of the most recent edition possible, since so many poetry outlets and publishers change addresses fairly frequently. Your local library will be able to order copies for you to borrow if they do not already have the books on their shelves.